THE LOVIST

Investigations and Poetry on Love and Death

Evan Costa

CONTENTS

Title Page
Preface
Other Cultures and Their Conceptions — 1
Entropy, Love, and Life — 17
A Novel Definition — 26
Consciousness and Love — 40
Insights on Art from a Novel love — 61
Investigating Érōs — 73
Relating to Philia — 84
Towards a Stronger Life Affirmation, a Deeper Philautia — 96
Life Performance with a Novel Conception of Love — 110
Miscellaneous Poems Found Floating at Dawn Upon the River — 134
The Lovist — 162
Citations — 163
About The Author — 165

Copyright © 2025 Evan Costa

All rights reserved

No part of this book may be reproduced, or stored in a retrieval system, or transmitted in any form or by any means, electronic, mechanical, photocopying, recording, or otherwise, without express written permission of the publisher.

ISBN: 9798311058919

Library of Congress Control Number: 2025902951

Imprint: Independently Published By Evan Costa

Cover Art: Samuel Prout (British, 1783–1852) "Mountainous Landscape with Bridge", 1814. The Cleveland Museum of Art, Gift of Mr. and Mrs. Herbert N. Bier, London 1954.648.f

Printed in the United States of America

PREFACE

*This work is dedicated to the many
who have illuminated my life
through their timeless works,
echoing in eternity.*

*All the great poetry—
inundated, translated—
carries a tragedy.
My native tongue
deserves more purity,
more clarity.*

*This is not poetry of some other language and age,
not refracted by the distorting mirrors
of some scholar's page.
The fruit of our culture,
A labor from modernity's time,
not some novel appropriation
of another's long past rhyme.*

*Ponder with heed, and be slow to read;
speak it aloud if you must.
Poetry teaches one not to rush,
your internal somber glow
will grow stunted when cultivated with speed.*

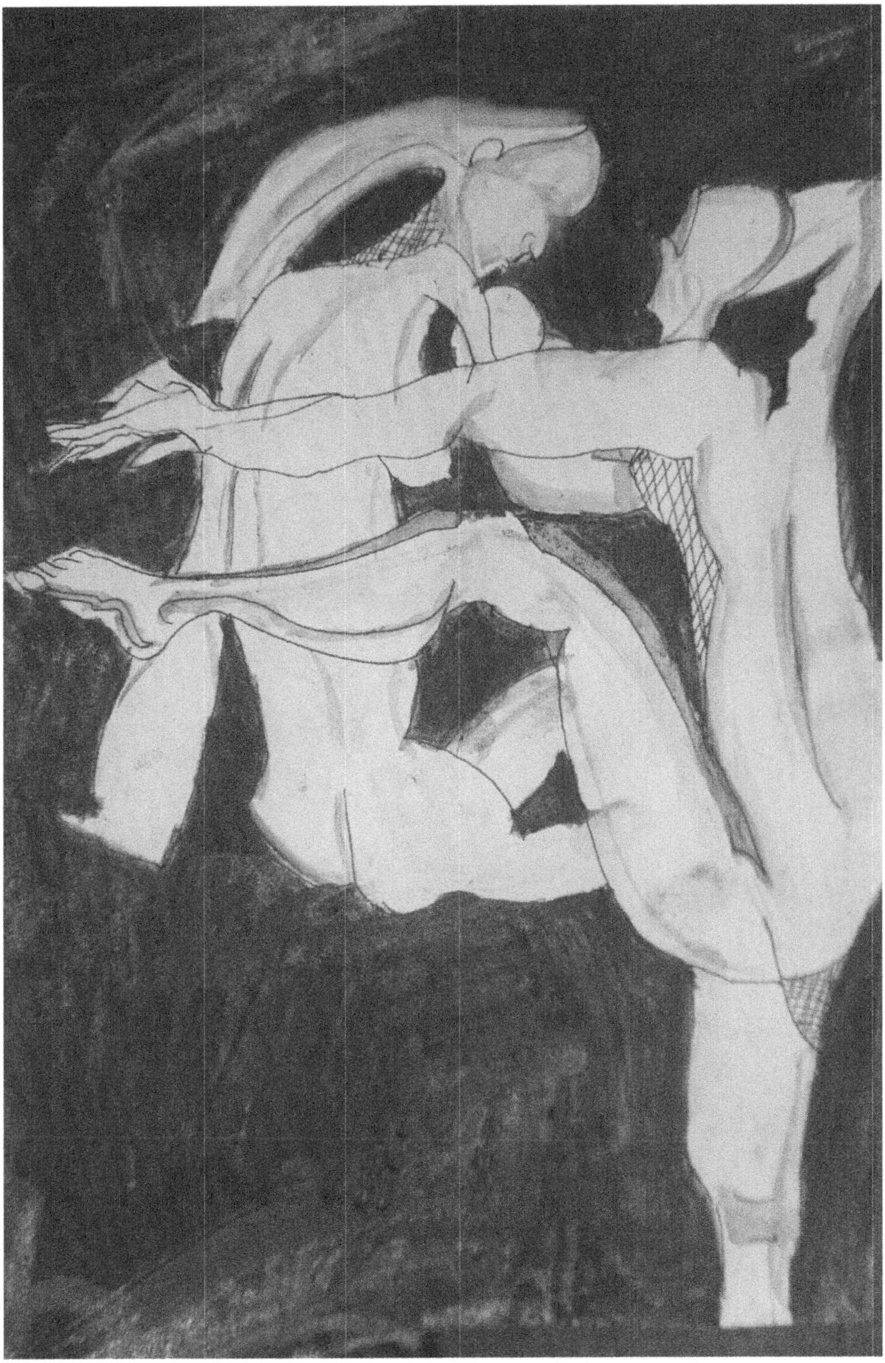

OTHER CULTURES AND THEIR CONCEPTIONS

Love, not something searched for and attained.
True love, oh so ever-present,
is what's left when nothing remains.

Language is not just the instrument through which we express thought—it is the forge where understanding itself is shaped. Without language, our representational understanding of the world unravels into instinct, a shadow of meaning. When words create reality, poetry turns the tides backward and makes the moon bleed crimson. Our minds, which comprehend only through classification and relativism, possess words as their ultimate tool. Without the representation of the external world through language, how would we perceive or understand reality beyond the instinctual responses dictated by biology? We might look at the lives of individuals with disabilities before the advent of sign language for insights, but even in these cases, the boundaries of understanding become blurred. Since language can be expressed in multiple forms—such as through body language and facial expressions—people who are unable to produce verbal language can still develop a functional understanding of their surroundings. However, in the absence of any interpretable information, the nature of the mind itself remains unknown. A plausible hypothesis, though, might be that without language, there is no conception of the self at all. Once a word is created, it demands a formalized definition, one that is often hastily assigned and left to fossilize as an accepted truth. Yet, a definition is always just a representation—merely a shadow of reality, a ghost. When the definitions are inconsistent with reality, they must shift, evolve, and transform until they converge to form an impression of sensibility. But even this process is inherently limited. We find ourselves in a precarious position, simultaneously dependent on words for structured communication and yet oppressed by their limitations. Linguistic primitivism obscures our understanding and diminishes the multisided coins of truth that shimmer to illuminate our reality. Linguistic poverty undermines the sophistication essential for higher thought. The word "human" predates our understanding of humans as a species. Our comprehension of humanity as a distinct group is shaped by the way we construct language. Just as language can draw distinctions between humanity and its surroundings, it can also collapse these boundaries, shaping our understanding profoundly depending on its construction. Once the phoenix is slain, from its ashes, perhaps daybreak anew.

Going on singing and dancing
quetzal feathers rain down
jade unearths at each stepping
Paying no attention
To the clouds thundering with strife
giving no heed
he pleases the giver of life.

The languages we speak today are not chosen purely through progressive evolution as Darwinian theories might suggest. Instead, linguistic change resembles the randomness of a complex system, shaped by cultural collisions, historical events, and chance.[1] For instance, when the Spanish arrived to conquer the Mesoamerican and Andean regions, epidemics had already dismantled the institutions of these cultures. Spanish supplanted indigenous languages not through inherent superiority but through the opportunistic dominance over fractured and weakened societies.[2] Through scholarship, we can grasp perspectives that capture ideas our own culture and language may have overlooked. The dice throw of life decides not only how we speak but how we behave and think. Although love manifests differently across cultures, depending on customs and values, it remains a core theme in literature and music, even in societies with oral traditions.[3] Systematic ethnographic, anthropological, literary, and neuroscience studies support the notion that romantic love is a universal human experience.[4] However, romantic love by itself offers no metaphysical insight, despite its centrality. Consider the richness or sparseness of a culture's vocabulary for love. Cultures with a single-word framework for love, like English, reflect a belief in the universality of love—a self-causative, infinite, and monistic metaphysical substance. This framework suggests that love in all its forms, whether romantic, familial, friendly, or universal, is fundamentally the same. While this simplicity invites poetic richness, it also poses challenges of concision, ambiguity, and miscommunication. For instance, in a single-word framework, clarity about the uniqueness of love may rely on descriptors or added clarification. While in other languages it would only require a single work, in English someone might say, "I feel a friendly love for you," if you want to specify a type of love, or elaborate a romantic love's depth with poetic imagery: "My love for you rumbles my heart like the shaking earthquake crumbles the world's buildings apart." These additions demonstrate that even single-word systems can capture complicated feelings by augmenting them effectively. Cultures with expansive vocabularies for love offer precision and clarity, equipping their speakers to articulate nuanced experiences and performances of love. Both approaches reveal truths about human connection, shaped by the linguistic tools available to us.

Those readily available books,
Whose substance and uniqueness
Are only accessed by the elite,

Whose critiques, so biting, in others would break teeth,
Whose richness cannot be matched,
Whose internal depth is so cavernous
It would drive a commoner to suicide, madness.

I met another who speaks my language,
Made me more ashamed as each passage turns whole.
A king aims to conquers bodies; the poet aims to conquers souls.

The ambiguity of a polysemous representation can infuse poetic expressions with profound richness, compelling readers to discern the context and form of love the poet conveys, whether it resides in its highest ideals or lowest manifestations. This ambiguity offers theoretical depth, allowing for layered interpretations. However, single-word frameworks for love also present drawbacks, such as issues of concision, miscommunication, and oversimplification. People may struggle to articulate the uniqueness of their love when limited to a singular term, risking a flattened or monolithic understanding of an experience that is inherently diverse. This limitation can shape perceptions, leading individuals to believe that love can only be expressed or performed in one particular way. Moreover, the absence of nuanced vocabulary can hinder individuals from realizing when extra clarification is necessary. In modern English, additional explanations beyond the phrase "I love you" are rare, with context performing much of the interpretative labor. This reliance on context can leave inexperienced lovers vulnerable to misunderstanding, as the single term does not always capture the multiplicity of feelings or intentions.

My love, the stars, they glisten so far.
I am afraid we are alone in this apparition,
which so violently splits the darkness.
We celebrate this stage, this theatre,
by dancing for another's pleasure.
I admit it is always better when we have each other,
when we dance together.
But even though I have you to hold and listen,
I must know why I still so deeply suffer.
For it is in the gravest moments of despair
that I created you from the love that drips off my heart's melting glacier.

I will never know you in truth, merely through my own interpretation.
For that reason, with or without your connection,
I will always be in deep isolation.

My love, the stars, they glisten so far,
yet what would they be without our perception?
The universe has created our inner light because it yearns to feel itself through us.
Existing as the burning white constellations was simply not enough.

While poetic ambiguity may enrich expressions of love, it also leaves room for misinterpretation, particularly for those who lack the experience or insight to navigate its subtleties. Such languages allow individuals to select terms that best fit their emotional nuances without leaving meaning ambiguous or open to interpretation. History teaches us that language, like love, is dynamic—constantly shifting, adapting, and reshaping our understanding of the world. In moments when language falters, poetry steps in to bridge the gaps, inviting us to feel meaning as much as we comprehend it. This interplay of precision and ambiguity, constraint and creativity, reveals that language's highest purpose lies in illuminating the human experience in all its intricate complexity.

I assume that a richer vocabulary is a result of competitive necessity. Interestingly, just as Inuit has many terms for love, they also have about ten distinct terms to describe subtle differences in ice. A rich vocabulary for a topic often reflects its cultural and environmental importance. Just as how for the Innuits in the deep tundra, knowing the specific type of ice can mean life or death— depending on the competitiveness of love in certain cultures, knowing the difference between types of love can also mean life and death. Some types of ice can cause you to fall into water and drown while other types are ideal for constructing igloos. Knowing the specific type of love a person is experiencing can determine if you want to grow or end a relationship. In ancient Greece, where violence and killing are integral parts of life, knowing how a romantic interest feels specifically can help understand if they are worth pursuing even if there are oppositional familial or political pressures to not pursue them, in other words pursuing certain people romantically can often place a person's life at serious risk. In the case of virtuous love knowing what types of love a king or general is driving his decisions will determine if they are worthy enough to support. Following the right King with the right character and virtues can also mean life and death on the battlefield or in the political operations of a state. Just as some cultures are war-like, there are other cultures that are more love-like. A love-like culture would drive specificity and technicality in language to avoid making errors. Just as a war-like culture would have jargon for tactics, strategies, historical precedents, literary allusions, words for identifying situations, a love-like culture will have jargon that is just as ubiquitous.

Dreary tavern,
the kind that sells all spirits.
I usually ignore them,
walk past their signs—
darkness where the grape
transforms to wine,
just as solitude has changed mine.

A common plot format in works of literature involve main characters committing suicide, or doing some self-destructive action because of a miscommunication, ambiguity, or misunderstanding related to romantic love. Since there is no distinction made between playful love or serious "I want to be with you at all costs" love, or rational love as in "you are perfect relationship for my current situation, but the relationship negatively impacts me I will move on" characters are left in turmoil and despair as they do not understand the actions of their beloved. For example, if one character feels for another the grave romantic love: "We should be together at all costs" while another feels a playful romantic love: "We should flirt and find pleasure in the relationship while we can," both people will say "I love you" to each other yet have deeply different meanings as to what their "I love you" entails. Then when the "We should be together at all costs" lover goes to a bar or a workplace and sees the "we should have fun together" lover flirting with another person then they are left feeling betrayed and heart broken. If, however, both lovers used a different term which captured the gravity of love while illustrating the differences in expectations about how it should be performed then it would provide clarity to both lovers about the intricacies of each other's feelings. This would save people from much emotional distress in the future if implemented correctly.

I expect some readers to say if you feel a playful kind of love that is not true love and you should say instead "I feel affection for you" not "I love you," but affection is not love. True love can take many forms even if it does not conform to your expectations. Love, even when playfully performed as a game, can still be built from the same profundity of eternal love. In English, while you can add a description to the type of love or add poetry to capture how the loving feeling is unique for you in a certain situation you cannot truly replace the word "love" in a sentence without losing something powerful in its meaning. For example, this communicates how destructive and life-changing a love is, but without the added words to love you would not know how my love is unique compared to the dry theoretical form of the default definition. You can replace use terms like affection, endearment, fondness, liking, lust, infatuation, devotion, but these are not forms of true love they are lower in the hierarchy of love. Love tends to be monarchic as the one true word for the mystical and profound idea. For example, the statement "I feel affection for you" or "I adore you" or "I am infatuated with you" are more related to trivial feelings rather than the grave seriousness embedded into the statement "I love you." One day we will have terms just as profoundly serious as "I love you" that also add color as to what kind of love one is talking about. A playful love, which can be still serious in its commitment to playing? A familial love, that describes the confirmation of loyalty that is expected culturally from a blood relation. These may require different words.

If I get the fundamentals right
I can build a featherbed of a life,
The problem is it's not enough,
To be pampered and carried by the scruff,
My house of brick yearns to replace itself with marble
And the ego equally craves to push its designation mortal,
A long path to finally turn to letters and texts,
All there is when there is nothing left,
And what is the price
For exaltation at the typewrite?
paid with a soul's brutish kicks and shoves,
marble is primarily bought with blood.

Why should I tell a family member the same phrase "I love you" as I would say to a girlfriend? Shouldn't there be different words to highlight those different types of love? I will not use the "I adore you" or "I am infatuated with you" simply because that is not how I am feeling. If I told someone I love them, and they told me "I adore you" or "I am infatuated with you" in return, even though those statements convey a stern intensity of emotion, I would be disappointed. I want to hear "I love you" back, a negation, or nothing at all in the cases that my love is unrequited. No other word will suffice, in fact to some degree I will feel hurt if another uses some other word than love as a replacement.

To compare different conceptions and definitions of love in different cultures and languages let's first evaluate the polysemous definition of love in English:

1. Deep care, attachment, and intimacy for a family member or personal tie
   a. Parent, child, friend, pet
2. Attraction and sexual desire for a romantic interest
3. Strong devotion, attachment based on qualities of a subject or object
   a. Love of playing guitar, love of strawberries, love of an actor or doctor
4. Unselfish, virtuous love for well-being of a subject or object
   a. Love of God, love of the world

Beyond those core definitions there are a few other usages that are not relevant like for example calling someone "My love" as a phrasing of option 1, or love in the context of tennis. From these definitions we can see that love is very important to the English language because of how widely it can be applied. The definitions capture how love can be directed at anything from people to places, physical objects, or experiences. However, even though love in English is polysemous it is easy to grasp how it is used in different context. Love is not necessarily used to provide colorful elaboration, but used to illustrates the intensity of depth of feelings.

The definitions of loves in an Ancient Greek context involve the following:[5]

1. Μανία (Manía) – Frenzied, obsessive love.
2. Ἔρως (Érōs) – Love associated with ideal beauty or passionate desire.
3. Λούδος (Lúdus) – Playful, game-like love.
4. Στοργή (Storgē) – Familial or affectionate love.
5. Ἀγάπη (Agápē) – Altruistic, unconditional love; love for all.
6. Πρᾶγμα (Prâgma) – Practical, enduring love.
7. Φιλία (Philia) – Deep friendship or platonic love.
8. Φιλαυτία (Philautia) – Self-love, either healthy or excessive.

The types of love from Ancient Greek appear to be constructed such that they can be applied leniently in different contexts. For example, Érōs seems like it can be used in the contexts of sexual attraction and loving a beautiful art piece. The eight terms seem to synthesize with the 4 polysemous definitions of English in a straightforward way. Manía, Érōs, and Lúdus, seem to all be commonly associated with romantic, sexual love. If someone is crazy or obsessive, amazed by a person's beauty, or diligently flirtatious with someone else, then it would be normal to claim they are in love in English. Storgē and Philia falls in the first definition of English love relating to family and friendship and Agápē falls within the fourth definition relating to virtuous and altruistic love. Since the definition of Philia captures platonic love, it would also include loving experiences, objects or places, falling into the third definition for English love.

It makes for a stale world when everyone's the same.
One day we will wake up and see how deeply runs our shame.

Too much pleasure, and it ruins the poetry.
To write well, one must suffer appropriately.

For example, using the verb form Philô of Philia, you could express in Greek how you love to play the lyre, which would carry the meaning that you have a platonic love for the object and experience. Prâgma is not captured within the English language, as a modern human would see utility and love to be separate concepts. Philautia is not captured by a single word in English, but the concept is expressed with self-love or loving one-self. Greek has this sense of simplification, reduction, clarity, which is a common theme within the western cultures that follow from their example. *Shallow, but shallow out of profundity!*

Below are a list of some of the core words for love in Arabic.[6][7]

1. Tattim (تطم): Love that captures the heart. "Stolen my heart."
2. Hawa (هوى): The intensity of love that brings inherited grief. "Love-sick"
3. Shaghaf (شغف): Love that nestles itself deep in the heart and is difficult to take out.
4. Sababah (صَبَابَة): Love that oozes out of your skin, makes you

feel queasy.
5. Ishq (عشق): Unconditional love that is always is and will be true.
6. Teeh (تيه): Love in which you lose control and a sense of yourself. Crazy or madly in love with someone.
7. Walah (وله): Love that carries sorrow, where intense affection leads to heartache or lovesickness.
8. Gharm (غرم): Love that demands sacrifice, a devotion that comes with a cost.
9. Hayaam (هيام): Love that drives one to madness, overwhelming reason and consuming the lover entirely.
   10. Hubb (حب): The foundational love that settles in the heart and endures.
   11. Wadd (ود): A steadfast, loyal love that remains constant over time

Arabic appears more descriptive about love than Ancient Greek and is more poetic in some ways. It is profoundly different of its conception. The Arabic form of love seems to focus on the experiential uniqueness. It almost seems as if a doctor is classifying different diseases with symptoms to make a corresponding diagnosis and treatment. For example, Hawa, Shaghaf, Sababah, Teeh, Walah, and Hayam all seem to have different psychological or physical ailments that incumber health. Whether love infects its victim in the heart or on the skin. Arabic has no hesitation with its poetic nature. Tattim is a mixture of Manía and Érōs. Wadd is like Prâgma, however even though Shaghaf also can be included it has a touching uniqueness. Shaghaf is different in that it seems to convey the lover did not want to fall in love, but love found its way inside them like a parasite. Overall, the different words for love offered by Arabic resonate with my personal experiences relating to love.

Scholars generalize Tamil literature to have 3 main categories for love in Tamil love poems called "akam poems." [8] Most of Tamil literature revolves around Aintinai, which vividly connects love themes to the environment and terrain.

The definitions are listed below

1. Kaikkilai (கைக்கிளை): Unreciprocated or one-sided love.

2. Peruntinai (பெருந்திணை): Mismatched or deviant love.
3. Aintinai (ஐந்திணை): Canonical love types, associated with specific landscapes and emotions.
    a. Kurinji (குறிஞ்சி):
        i. Landscape: Mountainous regions.
        ii. Theme: Represents the joyful and secret union of lovers in a romantic setting.
    b. Palai (பாலை):
        i. Landscape: Desert or wasteland.
        ii. Theme: Reflects the sorrow of separation and the hardships of love during journeys or obstacle
    c. Mullai (முல்லை):
        i. Landscape: Forest or pastoral regions.
        ii. Theme: Symbolizes patience and longing as a lover awaits their partner's return.
    d. Neidal (நெய்தல்):
        i. Landscape: Seashore.
        ii. Theme: Depicts wailing and grief caused by betrayal or obstacles in love.
    e. Marutam (மருதம்):
        i. Landscape: Agricultural or riverine regions.
        ii. Theme: Represents quarrels or playful conflicts between lovers in a domestic setting.

Kaikkilai and Peruntinai are used scarcely in Tamil literature perhaps because they are seen as scandalous forms of love. For example, Kaikkilai when contrasting infatuation and indifference can often result in the unreciprocated love becoming hateful, reckless, or self-destructive.

The crack of lightning,
splitting eternal darkness—
Should we not
act in accordance?

Representing the uglier side of love. Peruntinai is used to describe a loving relationship that breaks social or cultural norms like between two lovers with a large difference in age, class, culture. Peruntinai would also include relationship outside of heterosexual norms. These expressions of love, while being facts of everyday life, are difficult to write about especially in a political milieu that suppresses taboo topics, one can see why the Tamil poets stick to esoteric landscapes.

There are languages that separate love out into two concepts like in Japanese and Hindi. Where there is one term for romantic relational love "pyaar" (प्यार) in Hindi and "koi" (恋) in Japanese, with another term "ai" (愛) and "prem" (प्रेम), which is a more spiritual unconditional "true" love. In Japanese, you can combine both words "Renai" (恋愛)". Japanese is a more unique conception, perhaps since it is born outside the Indo-European yoke, and is more hierarchical by nature than other languages. In the beginning stages of a Japanese relationship a couple might use the words "suki desu" (好きです), which signifies liking someone. Then as the relationship matures into a loving marriage one might use "aishiteru" (愛してる). Japanese culture verbally expresses "I love you" rarely compared to how often it is used in Western cultures.[9] The custom of verbally expressing love infrequently is a commonality amongst many countries, and is just as common as the Western tradition around the world.

Like milk to the baby,
and honey to the mature,
to a soul arid and impure,
moisture forms gently.
What brings life its humble allure?
The droplets of love, and their muted hues,
that flicker faintly on the pasture's dew.

Western cultures see love as lasting forever Eastern cultures see love as temporary, and often use the metaphor of a flower to symbolize love's beauty and limited lifespan. While, Eastern cultures have a subtle suspicion with love as deceptive and dangerous. Western cultures see love as unequivocally positive and noble; they see real love as lasting forever – we can see here why the polysemic single-word form of love is the preferred representation by the West as the Western conception believes all love as one and eternal.

The interesting part of comparing eastern and western differences in love's conception is that while they are profoundly different both produce examples of upstanding and noble relationships. Part of the difficulty as well is that the terms "Eastern" and "Western" categories of cultures are generalizations that do not truly capture the diversity of cultures around the world. Perhaps a better way of capturing the dichotomy of love in the world's cultures are through comparing individualistic and collectivistic cultures.[10] In individualistic cultures, love emphasizes personal freedom, emotional intimacy, and verbal expression, with relationships often ending if expectations aren't met. In collectivistic cultures, love is shaped by family and social ties, prioritizing altruism, friendship, and actions over words. In countries like Poland and Russia, love is viewed through passion, altruism, and efforts to improve a partner's well-being. However, Americans valued comfort and friendship, viewing love pragmatically. Collectivistic cultures see love as more negative or an unreal fairy tale that either fades or evolves into long-term friendship. For this reason, Poland despite being rooted geographically inside Europe more closely resembles Japan and China in their conception of love than they do their more individualistic German neighbors

Look at all that glittery gold
on your heavy chains and filled coffers.
But the feather is heavier
on the scale when your heart is offered.
So much money worth everything you hold,
But your soul's texture is like
old paper creased with careless folds.

Along with work to identify collectivism and individualism there are decades of scholarship classifying cultures into low context or high context communication customs and verbal reticence. Verbal Reticence signifies how verbally reserved a culture is. For example, the United States and Germany are both low context individualistic cultures that necessitate more verbal expressiveness, but Germany has much higher reticence. This causes cultural distinctions in that Germans may be slower to develop relationships, and more precise in communication, while U.S. culture may seem more outgoing and emotionally expressive. However, in Chinese high-context culture verbally saying "I love you" often or expressing your personal emotional complexities relating to a relationship would be perceived as unusual.[11]

Beyond the definitions provided earlier, here are some honorable mentions whose concepts are not commonly expressed in English:[12]

1. Dor (Romanian): A deep yearning for a loved one.
2. Flechazo (Spanish): Instant attraction or love upon first meeting.
3. Geborgenheit (German): The comforting sense of security when with loved ones.
4. Oodal (Tamil): Playful, lighthearted fighting between romantic partners.
5. Iktsuarpok (Inuit): The anticipation and desire to see someone again.
6. Onsra (Boro): The bittersweet feeling that love is fleeting and won't last.
7. Yuanfen (缘分, Chinese): The mysterious force or destiny that brings people together.
8. Forelsket (Danish): The euphoric feeling of being in love.
9. Manabamate (Rapa Nui): The lack of appetite that comes with falling in love.
10. Gezelligheid (Dutch): The cozy warmth of being surrounded by loved ones.
11. Kilig (Tagalog): The thrilling, dizzy sensation felt when seeing a lover.
12. Odnoliub (Однолюб, Russian): A person who experiences one true love in their life.
13. Hai shi shan meng (海誓山盟, Chinese): The belief in eternal, undying love.
14. Naz (ناز, Urdu): The pride and satisfaction felt from being loved.

The definitions provided above are all rich, and delighting to learn about, but they give a sense as if they cannot exactly hit the bullseye on what is truly love. They define emotions, feelings, sensations, how the love is expressed, or by identifying the object of that love. Some definitions approach the attributes and potential representations of love. However, they have not precisely defined love itself. Everyone describes love in metaphor, symbol, or imagery, but keep their distance in directly identifying love as if it is some illusive spirit or mythical monster. For example, Storgē is defined by its direction toward family or by its distinction from sexual love. Yes, it is love directed toward this defined subject, but what is the definition of the love I am directing? Care and intimacy as definitions are inadequate to define true love. We both know all too well the many situations marked by excesses of care and intimacy, yet utterly barren of true love. After considering all the definitions, one might think, "I understand this is a type of expression of love; this is love toward a specific aspect of life," but we still have not answered what love itself is, which has eluded poets and philosophers for many millennia. When creating a more robust or dynamic philosophical framework, the greatest minds merely skirt around the topic. It is peculiar that love is so infrequently discussed when it is so fundamental to our existence. The philosophers sometimes show that they know more but only communicate their understanding in between the lines in short flashes. They create webs of understanding but love always belongs to the framing threads and auxiliary spirals. Where philosophers show a clear conception of eternal love, their discourse often feels tangential to their original points. The philosophers treat the subject as just another phenomenon of existence, distinct from their broader metaphysical valuations as if they are encountering an elephant for the first time while blindfolded. Those investigators discover love in various contexts and express surprise at its pervasive presence. The psychologists have attempted to conceptualize love formally too; however, their conceptualizations only focus on romantic love. They create rigorous explanations for romantic love because it is something you can collect data on, something you can statistically analyze and quantify! However, true love is not as easily quantified by surveys and brain scans, and romantic love is only a component of the multi-faceted usage in the English language. Conceptualizing a component of love is inadequate for understanding the bigger picture.

Has this world become devoid of love's respect
In accordance with millennia long intellectual neglect?
The words, the language, the desert that forgets,
Waiting for something new, all left of them residue,
For when books are burned, people are burned too.

ENTROPY, LOVE, AND LIFE

The difficulty in defining love reflects a broader challenge in understanding life itself—both are marked by complexity and resistance to simple explanations. Just as love eludes precise characterization, life operates within hierarchical systems driven by physical and biological laws. To grasp the essence of love, one must also engage with the underlying structures of existence, where complexity, entropy, and the inevitability of struggle are fundamental truths. Everywhere one investigates life, hierarchies and pyramidal structures emerge—similar to the pyramids that captivated our ancient architectural predecessors. In ecosystems, as organisms stratify themselves into trophic levels, biomass decreases due to energy transfer inefficiencies, with only a fraction of energy moving up the chain. Organisms at higher levels tend to be less numerous, often more predatory, and sometimes more complex, reflecting the inherent constraints of these systems. Biomass at each level in the food chain is driven by the most fundamental laws of physics. The free energy trapped in biomass at each transfer is lost to entropy as defined in the second law of thermodynamics. Free energy is not only lost when energy is transferred from one organism to another but is also lost from organisms simply living. Life is a fight for free energy against the forever increasing entropy of the universe. Black holes were our only hope for a physical phenomenon that can produce indefinite free energy; however, that dream of negative entropy was disproven with Hawking radiation. The futile fight of life against the laws of physics is what makes life as suffering an empirically consistent and obvious statement given the evidence. For as much as a biological entity suffers to achieve their evolutionary drives: self-preservation, reproduction, and growth, over the long term we, as in all life, must be destroyed by ever-increasing entropy. We are designed to try as hard as possible to win at a game that we are pre-determined to lose. It is possible that once entropy equilibrates in the Big Freeze —where no free energy remains and life becomes unsustainable—it could eventually reverse into a state of contraction, leading to the Big Crunch, with life unfolding in reverse.

Time will pass ... pass and pass.
And, oh, so much will make no sense,
without that special compass,
the pulling of love's presence.

The universe will then move infinitely in a state of expansion and contraction, which would imply the universe has had this property for all of eternity forward and back. It is also possible that the entropy reversion phase of the universe does not match the exact inverse of the current our forward moving reality. Thus, in eternity every version of matter in every possible combination and permutation must necessarily exist at one point as the universe is eternally expanding and contracting also known as Eternal oscillation or the Oscillating Universe Theory. This is how eternal recurrence can be rooted in modern physics, and an eternal framework for viewing the universe has more reason than the Big Bang, since time will exhibit properties that are unknowable and unprovable when the universe is in a singularity phase prior to expanding. Whether entropy will increase forever or forever oscillate, both indicate that any pursuit of the natural inclinations of life, such as procreation or self-preservation, are pointless endeavors. If the universe equilibrates to entropy death, then any advantage will ultimately be meaningless after death. If the universe eternally oscillates than as every version of reality is necessitated if you work too be successful there will be infinite versions of you that are unsuccessful and if you are unsuccessful there are infinite versions of you that are successful. Every point of probability to your advantage that you win in one reality you will lose in another since all realities necessarily have existed, exist already, or will exist. So, trying to accomplish a goal or win at something in this reality forces you to lose in another reality. Why try when trying does not in any way change your fate? Why should someone willingly participate in life? Why should someone play the futile game of dice destined to doom? Well... love is why.

Concentrated, condensed,
Poetry is amplified by solitude.
Other humans, their influence,
Always, dilute and delude.

It seems that we are only aware of suffering once we become aware of ourselves, as differentiated from our external environment. It is a human assumption that humans are individual entities that are separate from everything around us. If we were one with everything we would not suffer since everything is not necessarily degrading, as energy cannot be destroyed, only we are degrading relative to everything else as a transient materialization of energy. Thus, it is self-evident that consciousness, or an adequate conception of the separated self, is the cause of suffering. Since being conscious of oneself is to understand that one is degrading relative to the environment, or that one is inevitably dying, and that is the cause of suffering.

Thy cup may overrunneth on occasion.
Countless times a day must I reconcileth
what hath left me so chasten'd,
So much time to self subdue,
Finally, mine bowl hath overrunneth too.
For what is true always leaveth me bitter,
Until I saw the boy drinking at the river.
Water seepeth from his hands all different ways,
Kneeling at the road unpaved,
to the bowl, saw so clear I, thou art a slave.

So there are two alternatives we have currently to combat the conclusion of nihilism when facing our doomed fate. The first, is to remove consciousness, which is already spiritually understood through Buddhist nirvana and the deindividuating into oneness with the universe. The second option is to change our conception and emotions around the purposes of life. Given that some of purposes of life are to self-preserve, procreate, and increase one's own power, these purposes are futile to the increasing entropy of the second law of thermodynamics. These life purposes we hold close to our heart, our conception, and our preferences only because they are biologically preprogrammed within ourselves. The growing plants, the busy ants, just the same as humans all behave and act in accordance with this biological programming. Not by chance but because in many cases the same exact genetic sequences are being executed between species. However, there is no evidence that other species suffer, since there is no evidence they are conscious or have an adequate understanding of themselves as separated from the environment. For example, a stone sitting on the ground does not understand itself as separate from the environment, it has no self conception, and is not conscious, so it is incapable of suffering. Thus, if something does not perceive its own degradation it can not suffer, like the common saying "ignorance is bliss". If self-conceiving, degrading lifeform sees life not through genetic programming, but beyond self-preservation, beyond procreation, beyond acquisition of power, one can live life free from life's purposes and then death or existential futility do not cause suffering. Since one is not seeking or caring for self-preservation, death is not an oppositional force to one's existence, and since there is not conflict between desires and reality there is no suffering. Art is not well understood because most humanity is well ingrained within its own biological programming and art has no utility to serve life's purposes, it exists for itself, without a clear reason to its observer. It exists simply because it wants to exist, and it does not care if it perishes, or if its existence is futile. This philosophy: the obstinacy of the artful, is the ultimate rejection of nihilism, the ultimate contempt for suffering, and the final maturing of thought capable by life such as it approaches divine perfection outside of the material realm.

Love's deserved elucidation,
Not given by my predecessors' hands,
Whose giant palms,
I have for so long,
Failed to climb upon and stand.

As perception approaches the top of the pyramids of life, the forms get increasingly more complex and powerful in a biological arms race. The arms race that is the direct result of life forms behaving in accordance with life's purposes and its corresponding genetic programming. The arms race that is the exact materialization of perpetual suffering. Also known as the Red Queen Hypothesis in evolutionary biology referencing to Alice and Wonderland where the queen is running as fast as possible but staying in place. Let us take for example, take a life pyramid with grass as the primary producer, rabbits as the primary consumer, and hawks as the secondary consumer. As the grass grows it's a relatively straightforward biological process, turning the free energy of sunlight into hydrated carbon that can later be used as energy to fight increasing entropy. Towards the top of the hierarchy of animals, where humans are, there are increasing number of preconditions for existence. With the human being as one of the most difficult animals to develop, something like grass at the bottom of the pyramids only has a relative few preconditions to exist like nutrients, decent climate, and water. Weeds as a type of grass can grow in the cracks of cement, and if there is limit on how well a blade of grass can do with its luck, it just produces seeds to spread and find a better environment elsewhere growing again by scratch without any subtleties and inconveniences involved in growing animals. The rabbit, a direct animal above the food chain of grass, has more preconditions than grass, since it eats grass it has all the preconditions for grass plus all the preconditions specific to the rabbit's existence. For example, a rabbit may need a hole to burrow in as shelter while grass can grow almost anywhere that meets its few necessities, even in the smallest cracks of rocks. Rabbits need time to breastfeed and rear their young, with a litter of a couple rabbits. While grass can produce hundreds to thousands of seeds per plant. Existing as a blade of grass is orders of magnitude easier than being a rabbit in terms of serving the purposes of life.

If it does not rain,
the grass does not grow,
All experience pain,
but the ones fighting at the top,
will be the first to go.

This is a mechanic process that has limited complexity compared to higher order organisms. Additionally, there are fewer requirements for grass to sustain its own existence. Thus, being a blade of grass is much more expedient than being a hawk, since all grass needs, is some good soil, some sunlight and water and it can serve all of life's purposes easily such as procreation and self-preservation. Since grass has the most contact with free-energy, it is capable of procreating through spreading large quantities of seeds, and since grass can spread through the environment so rapidly it does not have to take serious action to self-preserve since it is orders of magnitude more difficult to eradicate every blade of grass in a particular area then it is, for example to kill the few hawks that inhabit a region. Grass is less powerful, less complex, but ironically harder to kill overall. In other words, as things get more complex they also get more precarious. Rabbits are at all of the same life risks as grass for example, disease, predation, environmental disturbances, mating issues, genetic discrepancies, but since they are more genetically complex they have more risk for genetic issues, and because they instead of being reliant on sunlight they are reliant on plant matter which has a much lower free-energy availability compared to sunlight, there is significantly less sustenance availability, and significantly more risk for genetic issues to occur compared to a more simple organism. This increases at the same degree as you move up each step with mice, snakes, and hawks.

Top predators having the most precarious position because they are reliant on every step in the food chain being healthy for them to have ample sustenance at the top. The hawk's children require more care than the rabbits despite rabbits being breast feeding mammals due to hawks having a more complex developmental process. Hawks also have smaller clutch sizes than rabbit litters because the are at such an advanced stage in the food chain that the amount of bioavailable free energy in rabbits is far more limited than the availability of sunlight or grass. So as food diminishes, there are higher biological risks due to genetic complexity, and life is generally harder as you move up the food chain. This is also seen with human beings, where as a human moves up the hierarchy of socioeconomic class that become an increasingly targeted person in by others to be harmed. A regular person who lives a humble lifestyle and minds their own business is far less likely assassinated than a societal leader or an aristocrat. It seems that as supremacy of an organism increases so does the precariousness of their existence. All of this begs the question why would any organism adapt itself to be further up the food chain? If there are no benefits, and only drawbacks, why would any organism adapt itself in this way?

From all the conquerors, nothing remains
other than their dissolving bones in the grave.
Though they have helped many roads get paved,
Their written stories will eventually morph and degrade.
From the poets, some remnants are left alive,
Seared into memory without a compare belied,
Untouched in perfection what was written in blood,
Burning from the unhealed injuries of love.

Could this perhaps be an instance of Will to Power? Where there is natural underlying genetic programming that not only favors life's purposes but also favors increasing complexity and capability. Though this explanation does not account for why certain organisms remain simple and powerless while others grow rapidly complex and powerful. Could it be that certain organisms become locked into a looping arms race cycle, causing a fiercely rapid adaptation toward increasing complexity and power? While other organisms never get looped into the cycle, they never experience pressures to grow more complex. The arms race loop would negate the Will to Power since it suggests that the increasing power of organisms is not an intrinsic biological phenomenon but a reaction to environmental pressures. We see many occurrences al throughout history of organisms making no evolutionary progress over millions of years of shifting conditions. If the Will to Power is not referencing biological mechanisms, but a larger metaphysical will, then where do we see growing power of compositions of energy and matter anywhere else in the universe other than life? The arms race hypothesis would also suggest Will to Life as a more appropriate philosophical framework, since every adaptation by an animal to increase power is an adaptive reaction of the organism to retain its life as the environment pressures it to die. The critique of Will to Life is: why would a living thing need to will itself into existence if it already exists, if it is already alive? It is true that an organism is thrust into life without necessarily willing it. Perhaps you can argue that the organism, once created, is the result of a Will to Life from its parental creator. A human baby may not be born from its own Will to Life, but from its parents' Will to *continued* life beyond themselves. Then, once an organism is thrust into existence, it must *continually* will to retain its existence. If it neglects or rejects this will, it will cease to exist. If an organism neglects its will to retain existence, it can stop eating or stop caring for itself, which will cause it to die.

In the moonrise,
there go again your sad eyes.
When wherever life seems ordinary,
that crescent moon jumps out high,
and stares at me ominously.
Those shouting eyes; daily,
I repent falling for the crude disguise,
that magic is not core to our reality.

If an organism rejects outright its will to continued existence it can commit suicide in some way. Perhaps the neglect of the self into death shows that suicide may not necessarily be a binary but on a spectrum. When we are threatened softly with death's hymns we are subtly alarmed with the strings of lyres in our hearts, the strings can be muted by a natural death drive. Facing mortal dangers with a melancholic nonchalance is a suicide all the same. For example, a deer being hunted by a wolf, can run a little slower because it is subtly tired of its own existence, this small performance of spiritual exhaustion can be a performance of suicide that is lower on the spectrum than a human overtly shooting themselves. If an organism is capable of committing suicide, then at every point of that organism's life there is *a choice*. The sacred choice of continuing to live to terminating one's life. Because every moment an organism is continually affirming its own existence, and not committing suicide, it is continually willing itself to life. Even though it is already alive the Will to Life is necessary for its continuance. Will to Power on the other hand is not necessary for an organism to live since so many organisms live in a way that over time, they in no way improve their genetic complexity or phenotypic capabilities.

Both Will to Life and Will to Power are affirmations of life. Will to Power reflects a nonsensical emergent property where organisms adapt to increase complexity and capabilities, despite the risks to self-preservation and reproduction. Will to Life, on the other hand, involves an organism affirming its existence, even when suicide could end its suffering—assuming the organism possesses self-perception that induces natural suffering.

*Listen closely when the trees speak,
You will find compared the human spirit weak.
Have you seen another group face death so nobly?
Of prejudices, I have never seen some so free.
The trees remain silent even in the worst tempests,
Because they love life and death equally.*

So, why be a hawk even though it is so precarious? Even though it is so much easier to be a blade of grass. Why be human, and be aware of our own transient existence, when we can be the blessed rock that does not know it exists and is thus incapable of suffering? These organisms exist despite their ignorance being fundamentally irrational because of love. Love is about affirming the irrational.
Just as by comparing different levels of organisms, we can see that some states of life are more irrational and unnecessarily difficult than others, we can generalize this observation to suggest that all of life is deeply irrational and nonsensical. The only rational suggestion so far has been to reach nirvana and oneness—which, let us not get confused, is a form of death and falls on the spectrum of suicide. Even the suicide rejector, the obstinate artist, is irrational, as they reject their own biological programming. So, why choose to exist when nonexistence is so much more rational, comfortable, and convenient? The only possible reason must necessarily be love. You must love—and I mean truly love—life to, after understanding all the facts that point to its futility, still desire to affirm it. Love is about affirming the irrational.

*When critiquing those who prematurely died,
"Their death was caused by pride"
Say many who think they're wise,
But those who condemn pride ,
Will never see how intrinsic it is to life,
Passing days by. To them, time is just to bide,
when their character so easily plied
every rule is something to abide,
they hide nothing but cowardice inside.*

A NOVEL DEFINITION

Life without deep love means that you did not deeply exist, as depth of love separates the ones who truly live from the mere passersby. An entity capable of understanding its own temporal degradation of itself and the necessitated degradation of all its posterity, yet still chooses to live is a choice made form the irrational, a choice made of love. Higher order intelligence is not necessary for love, as higher order intelligence is not necessary to choose life over death, it is merely a matter of taste or personal preference. A dumb person can choose to keep living while an intelligent person can choose death. Many intelligent people work themselves into intellectual circles that cause them to not understand love. Though an adequate conception of eternal love and its ever-flowing fountains will make suicide obsolete to the intellectual. Suicide after all is a tool. A tool to end suffering. The lover has contempt for seeing suffering as a negative notion. Rather the lover sees suffering as the essential test of their own ability to love.

Love's nature has this finality when used as an answer. The next question once we know love's importance is how we enjoy, beautify, and deify love to its fullest extent. We can now see some emerging details of truth about the nature of love. Since the hawk, by making its position more precarious, is diminishing its own progress towards the purposes of life, and because of its irrational existence relative to grass it necessitates greater love to affirm its own existence. Love is about affirming life and existence despite its irrationality and contradictory nature. A performance of love is when an organism acts outside of what is rational or acts outside of life's preprogrammed purposes. For example, if the purposes of life are to self-preserve, procreate then it makes more sense to be a simple organism like grass than it does a complex precarious hawk.

Thus, we can arrive to a better conception of what is love by the following propositions:

1. Proposition I: Life is the appropriation and expenditure of free energy for self-preservation, non-excessive reproduction.
    a. Corollary: When life is seeking advantage, growth, excessive reproduction, or expansion of capabilities and power, this is a result of hedging risks the life-form perceives to itself and its genetic lineage.
2. Proposition II: Love is the affirmation of existence independent of whether the approval supports or detracts from life's purposes.

To clarify, I separate our reproduction into excessive and non-excessive, meaning when an organism is reproducing to keep its lineage alive verses when an organism is reproducing to expand its genetic reach. Excessive reproduction would fall into an expansion of genetic reach in the Will to Power, while non-excessive reproduction would fall under normal Will to Life or will to continued existence. When exploring the different definitions provided for love in different cultures there was always this hint or suggesting that there is love, romantic and emotional, and there is true real unconditional eternal love. My novel definition defies that there is such a thing as false love. As in the romantic emotional expression of love is not love at all. It is better characterized purely as eroticism or romanticism. This is because emotions that carry desire purely for romantic partners fall into Proposition I in that they serve life's purposes. By attaining a desirable sexual or romantic partner you are following the directions of your genetic programming that is designed specifically for life. The desirable sexual partner provides healthy genetics for you as an organism to intermix and procreate with. Additionally, a partner can support you and help you do things you would not be able to by yourself, so in many ways your symbiotic relationship with them is improving your abilities for self-preservation.

Do not remit these showered gifts.
Love is not an emotion,
And a god is not spirit.
Do not tacitly degrade them
To approximation and representation.

Love, true love, as defined above is about caring for a partner beyond merely how they can help you in procreating and preserving yourself. So, if you partner turns ill, becomes unattractive, betrays you, or whatever undesirable thing occurs, you still love and affirm them regardless. If someone betrays you, for example, you can still take action to punish the behavior like stop talking to them, but if you stopped loving them for some reason then it would be conditional love, which is not true unconditional love stated in Proposition II. Additionally, feeling nervous around a beautiful person you would like to marry is not love, as the emotional response is a result of heightening the senses for what your brain perceives is important. Marrying a beautiful person is to your material advantage, improves your personal life, and wholly serves the purposes of material self-preservation. Nervousness or joy like other sensations mistaken for love, are merely material emotions. They are not true love because Love is when you care for another person regardless of if they are beautiful, love is the affirmation independent what is self-beneficial. That is difference of what is true love and what is false love. One is material and one is from beyond: the spiritual.

And many men who can do so much,
fight tooth and nail, kick and punch,
tell you every chemical composing nature,
work out math faster than calculators,
explain every detail of the stars above,
but cannot speak much on eternal love.

Another example, which should be common sense, is the relationship between parents and children. If parents support and care for their child only when the child is successful but withdraw that care during times of failure, this cannot be considered true love. In this context, success often aligns with serving life's broader purposes —such as achieving good grades, winning competitions, or other accomplishments that provide advantages in self-preservation and procreation. These successes can lead to better schools, higher-paying jobs, and stronger personal relationships. However, true love is unconditional. To truly love a child, parents must affirm and support them even when they fail—when they struggle to achieve, lack desirable traits, or face challenges that hinder self-preservation. Love cannot be contingent on performance or attributes. If certain aspects of the child cause rejection, then the child has not experienced genuine love from their parents. A childhood devoid of unconditional love can severely impair a person's ability to transform their parents' affirmation into their own unconditional affirmation of life. True love, by its nature, affirms a person regardless of their circumstances, behaviors, or qualities, forming the foundation for emotional and psychological well-being. The child is then restricted in their ability to transfer the love given to them into love of life, and since they only know a conditioned existence, once the conditions change to something irrational, they will be at a much higher likelihood to terminate their own life. Even if it is not performed directly, as said before suicide can be done on a spectrum of spiritual exhaustion. This is because life is irrational fundamentally and you need a lot of love to combat this irrationality and continually affirm life in its madness, but if you were never reared to develop your internal love then then you will not have the tools to reject suicide when suicide becomes expedient, which is unfortunately an inevitability at some point most lives.

A love not lascivious
Is a love that does not strike
My interest.
I present disgust to the phlegmatic,
And some unjust disappointment
At the mirror's sight,
For my inability to requite.

You may love me,
but do not expect reciprocity
of my whole capacity
if all you can muster is low in quantity.

A snake, which is often characterized as ruthless and soulless, is a prime example of an entity that serves life's purposes without any love. A snake is not truly present; it operates solely through biological drives designed to serve life's purposes and knows nothing beyond this mechanistic programming. It simply sees opportunities and strikes at them as they arise. The snake's only concern is its own advantage. Similarly, in the highest classes of human society, there will be fewer and fewer people capable of true love. Many only marrying each other for name or wealth. Reaching the upper echelons of society requires an intense focus on serving life's purposes. To rise to the top, one often has to "crack some skulls," and the traits of the parents are often passed on to their children. By successfully pursuing personal advantages—whether through money, power, or social relationships—you increase your status. However, dedicating all of your willpower to these pursuits risks neglecting love. Furthermore, there is the problem of life's conveniences: if you possess them, you will attract people who desire those conveniences. In such a situation, how would you ever know who truly loves you?

Why is love found in irrationality and inexpediency? Because rationality and expediency are used by organisms to find optimal paths to self-preservation and self-expansion. Organisms, without love, are merely robots that do what they are designed to do, and nothing more. Love on the other hand is what an organism can do beyond what they are naturally programmed. It is where the mechanistic conception of reality clashes with the truth of actual reality. There are generally two ideas that crush the soul's will, and they are derived the from physics and metaphysics outlined below from what was mentioned before:

1. Entropy equilibrates into certain death for all equally. All life comes to an end — into nothingness, and because all effort is transient it is meaningless.

2. Entropy reverses, once it fully equilibrates, into its antimatter equivalent. Life goes on forever or endlessly repeats in infinite recurrence forward and backward with every permutation of reality existing at some point in time.

For people awash in love either of these ideas are perfectly acceptable. If my life was short and meaningless at least you were a little flame of love within it before it ended. And if life goes on forever then you are eternal flame of love which lights the universe through self-causative affirmation of existence. Its own reward. Either way love makes the absurdity and existential dread of life insignificant. When man faces the jarring cliff of eternity. Man must face he has not consented to life and was thrust into it at birth. Forced to live with suicide as his only tool to truly escape it. How profoundly wretched are these truths? And, how trivial are these matters in the face of a true earnest love.

So be it true love rare,
Leaves me with more reason to prepare,
Makes more the error to fawn,
For there is long darkness before the dawn.
Perhaps the selfish are the wise,
As it provides the reason Athena
Condemns Odysseus for his truths,
And commends him for his lies.

One of the difficulties with there not being much writing on the intricacies of profound eternal love is that some people only understand love through romantic or erotic concepts, not only obfuscating true love but also misrepresenting eroticism and romanticism. Part of the aggressive prudence and chasteness espoused in our age is a result of a misunderstanding of love. People who do not understand how to fall in love or grow internal love naturally are afraid that a libertarian approach to sexuality might stunt the internal growth of love. They believe that if eroticism and love are opposing forces, the one to reduce should be eroticism rather than love. The truth is that both sexuality and love are completely independent of one another. You can have a wonderful sexual relationship completely devoid of love or a loving relationship devoid of anything sexual. Ideas like this, which to me are so obvious —and should be obvious to anyone—are apparently heretical to some. The aesthetic spiritualists, or people who never engage in sex, are constantly withholding themselves from earthly pleasures. These are the type who are emaciated from eating little, and everything they do lacks voluptuousness. These people have made such choices because they are searching for love, believing that earthly pleasures are oppositional to love—an unspoken and completely unfounded assumption that underpins their every decision.

Upper seventies in age,
in her later stages,
She needs help when walking up stairs.
The breeze on her flowing grey hair,
The sunlight shines,
for with her there is only perfect weather,
"You look beautiful" says her beloved,
as they walk the garden entranced together.
"Beauty?" the children ask doubtfully,
Looking at her wrinkles and frail body,
seeing two old fools wandering about pitifully.

We can further deduce from the new formed definitions of love some errors that are commonly held from assumptions about love. Statements like "But only God can grant love!" reflect a belief that we cannot decide when or how to experience love—a belief born of a soul long weakened and sickened by dependence on superstition. A person who cannot draw love from the deep wells of his own spirit waits idly for another to do it for him. Love has properties of both water and oil. It can nourish and sustain life, or it can poison and destroy it, turning fertile fields into barren wastelands. To believe oneself incapable of producing love is not humility; it is self-debasement. Love is not granted; it is created, cultivated, and performed.
The conflation of love with value is another grave error, treating it as a treasure to possess or a prize to win, reveals a misunderstanding of its nature. As something that should be evaluated as either "good" or "bad." Value and utility serve the purposes of life outlined in Proposition I, so any manner of value is not within the realm of love. This distortion is deeply embedded in language, especially in English, which is inherited from a maritime mercantile power, where love is intertwined with ideas of worth and merit. But love, in its essence, is neither a possession nor a currency. Love is not something to be appraised but something to be lived. The idea of searching for or finding love, as in the phrase "I was searching for love," is absurd. Love is not an external object to be found; it is already within you. To say you are "searching for love" is as nonsensical as saying, "I am searching for my brain." If you can articulate such a thought, it proves you already possess what you seek. Perhaps what people mean is that they are searching for a romantic relationship, a connection that transcends the ordinary and compels both partners to make

sacrifices in service of shared goals. This is not a search for love but for compatibility—a deliberate and rational pursuit. Finding the right partner requires discipline, effort, and openness, but it is not the same as searching for love itself. In truth, love is often impractical. Sometimes, the best choice for life's purposes may not involve love at all. To equate love with expediency is to misunderstand its nature entirely.

Questioning the existence of love, with statements like "Who is to say love even exists?" reflects a misunderstanding of its nature. Love does not exist in the material world, for it is not tangible. It is a construct of the mind and the spirit, a phenomenon shaped by your thoughts and beliefs. The existence of love is not dictated by the external world but by your willingness to believe in it and manifest it within your life. Love exists to the extent that you allow it to exist in your mind and actions. Its reality is yours to define. Reality is a chaos of absurd, uncorrelated, and independent events. Love has the remarkable ability to bring coherence to life, to make it make sense. You must decide: how much do you want your life to make sense? This is the same question as asking: how much do you want to love? Love has no measurable quality; only its quantity can be discerned.

They hope for the overman's thunder,
Dust settled from Apollo's chariot mustered.
So much to delight in the lightning and rain.
How can we wait for sunshine again?

Another grave error, akin to the error of love being searchable or findable, is the concept of finding or searching for happiness. The pursuit of happiness views happiness as an end goal; however, this notion is deeply unclear. If we define happiness as pleasure derived from fulfilling one's desires—desires that are reasonable, enduring, and not harmful—then because pleasure lies at the core of this definition, one remains enslaved to the chemical processes that induce it. Even if we adopt a more generous interpretation, where happiness is enduring fulfillment achieved by accomplishing one's desires, the question arises: why must fulfillment depend on achieving those desires? Someone can chase their dreams, wholeheartedly pursue their goals, and attain everything their heart desires while feeling deeply fulfilled throughout the journey. Happiness is not a reward that materializes only after desires are achieved; it is a state of being that a person is fully capable of choosing at any moment. To tie happiness exclusively to fulfilled desires is to gamble the quality of your life experience on factors often beyond your control. Desires may go unmet, circumstances may shift, and external conditions may fail to align with expectations, but none of these needs dictate your happiness.

What is the difference between a poem and a song?
Maybe one is meant to be short, while the other long?
Few can tell the difference, even when it's so clearly shown.
They both have rhymes, and little riddles so beautiful.
The difference is rarely found, for how it's so subtle.
One needs notes and sounds as a façade to its semblance,
the other lives self-assured, it will never know resemblance.
One is designed to joyously entertain,
the other owes only the writer any pleasure.
One needs a beat to keep it safe, sheltering,
the other has the universe knocking at its center.
So, what is the difference from a poem to a song?
The same difference between the king and the jester.
Both share much of the same in humanity,
suspended above their graves with thin sheets of sanity.
However, both experientially will know well within—
one lived a poem, and the other just a hymn.

The human mind operates at its clearest and most functional when it is rooted in a sense of enduring fulfillment—a fulfillment that stems not from external accomplishments but from a foundation of internal security and healthy self-esteem. Being unhappy before or while pursuing your desires can hinder your progress, clouding your judgment and sapping your energy. In contrast, choosing to be happy as you work toward your goals can often make you more productive and effective at achieving them. Why, then, do interpretations of the pursuit of happiness often assume that happiness must be postponed until desires are fulfilled? Such a notion ignores the human capacity to cultivate joy and contentment regardless of external conditions. By embracing happiness as a choice rather than a destination, one gains the freedom to live fully, regardless of what remains unaccomplished. Aiming to accomplish one's desires is an important part of a well-lived life. Perseverance and discretion, rooted in values like liberty, are also crucial but can only be fully realized by an educated mind.

The stars—they throw, sparkle, and shine,
    Look at the reflections in the darkness of my eyes.
There lies blackness that knows the midnight sky.
    Blackness has its depth and its layered hues,
    Blackness has more to discover and peer into.
For blackness knows the noon's twilight,
For blackness knows the cycling, surging, receding tide.

The more realistic interpretation of happiness emphasizes the pursuit of pleasure. The tenets of the pursuit of happiness—and its related concepts, such as individuality and liberty—have manifested in modernity in their most shallow forms. Modern cultures built on these ideas often prioritize fleeting gratification, materialism, and consumerism. This outcome is inevitable because pursuing enduring fulfillment and scrupulous desires requires rigorous education, which must be imparted by another person. In contrast, seeking short-term gratifications and unfulfilling pleasures is biologically ingrained, as it serves the immediate purposes of life. Rigorous education, however, demands reliance on a teacher, submission to authority, and the sacrifice of momentary pleasures in favor of discipline and study. Depending on another person for education contradicts individuality. Being under another's authority opposes liberty. Forsaking immediate pleasures to study undermines the pursuit of happiness. Is it not ironic that to attain enduring fulfillment, moral distinction, and higher reasoning, one must temporarily reject the values of individuality, liberty, and the pursuit of happiness? Instead, community, obedience, and pursuit of discipline. Happiness, as long as it is tied to pleasure or neurochemical components, will always vanish the more it is sought. If money is the condition for happiness, there will always be a desire for more. Even if something morally higher, like being well-read, becomes the condition for happiness, there will always be more books to read. Why tie happiness to a desire? Happiness is like a bird—hard to chase, but with the right bait and the right trap, it will come to you. Compared to love, happiness comes across as selfish and shallow. What if we lived in a world where people pursued love as an end in itself rather than chasing happiness? How much richer would our world be? Love is rooted in deeper and more enduring virtues; it is not as easily spoiled as happiness. I can endure any unhappiness for love, but the inverse is not possible.

Along with happiness, another error is the idea that love is predominantly expressed through caring or kindness. Caring for another is not inherently connected to their benefit, just as neglect is not inherently tied to harm. A person can grow stronger and more self-reliant when forced to care for themselves due to neglect. Conversely, a person's development can be stunted if they are never given the opportunity to care for themselves because someone is constantly doing it for them. The same applies to kindness. I will always prefer a friend who is authentic around me over one who is perpetually kind. The most valuable aspect of interacting with others is discovering what makes them unique—the qualities that make them irreplaceable. If everyone is molded into being uniformly kind, it diminishes their ability to act authentically. Encouraging kindness at all costs discourages people from following their internal compasses and acting in accordance with their true feelings. I would prefer a friend who is occasionally cruel or rude because such moments are human and natural. It makes me feel more comfortable and reassures me that my friend is a genuine person with emotions and complex behaviors, not a programmed robot always striving to be kind. When we define love without the concepts for caring and kindness intrinsic to the definition we encourage more complex and rich performances of love that may be difficult to understand in the short-term, but may grow more fruitful in the long-term.

They have perverted love
    To be kindness.
Let us spill each other's blood,
    Let it gush from our guts.
    In the steam that floats above
Reveals the true sacrifice
And mastery necessary.
    To forge the eternal gates of love.

The same intended ambiguity in love's novel definition applies to different human dispositions. For example, temperance, often seen as a more controlled and effective characteristic, may be seen as reasonably connected to deeper love. Some may consider temperance as a form of quiet, simple love. However, the benefits that philosophy and history attribute to temperance are related to life's purposes.

The effectiveness and stability associated with temperate people are linked to the advantages they gain in life due to their wise disposition. For example, a temperate captain is more likely to bring their boat safely back to shore. A temperate military officer is more capable of executing orders and succeeding in missions. These examples serve life's purposes, as they aim for self-preservation—not necessarily always for the officer or captain themselves, but for the people they work for or are responsible for. Love, on the other hand, is free from seeking advantage, self-preservation, self-expansion, or anything related to material life. Therefore, a person who is in every capacity intemperate, extreme, or excessive despite being harmful and ineffective at accomplishing goals is just as capable of performing and experiencing perfect love. Additionally, we have already discussed that serving life's purposes is a fruitless endeavor, as all advantages will ultimately disappear through inevitable entropy-death. While an extreme, unreasonable, or intemperate person may often be ineffective and harmful in serving life's purposes, they are the ones who create the best and most interesting art. It is radical art that captivates and inspires. Radical art that is the most interesting.

How maudlin the love poems past
How beautiful the pictures cast
All are formed with a subtle bitterness
Of whom they could not possess.
An underlying it all is mere simple sex.

Passion, on the other hand, can be an adequate expression of love. Just like in the pursuit of happiness, there is both a healthy and unhealthy expression of passion. When passion runs deep, enduring, and balanced, it combines intense emotions with the unconditional affirmation reminiscent of true love. Passion that is short-term and obsessive, however, may only be an emotional response that excites the brain when it sees a chance to gain an advantage or benefit. Not all passions are the same; some contain love, while others are devoid of it, depending on whether the passion is more emotional or spiritual. Passion, then, is no longer an adequate synonym for love, as we see that love is only a component of some forms of passion. The healthy form of passion will be long lasting, where material excitation is synchronized with real love. These types of passions usually lead to material success and the benefit of the person experiencing it.

If someone commits to actions that accomplish the goals and purposes of life, they are acting in accordance with their biological programming. This is often the healthiest thing for a person to do. After all, a person is a biological entity programmed by very specific genetic information. If a person seeks to reproduce, eat good food, make a lot of money, increase their own power, and so on, those are all things that are good and healthy for that person. However, having those desires is mechanistically programmed within our genetics. A person is not pursuing those desires out of love; they are pursuing them because they are biological machines programmed to do exactly that. However, because humans are capable of abstract thought, higher reasoning through the mind, and are conscious, we are also capable of doing things outside of our genetic programming. This is primarily what separates humans from machines. A machine will only ever act in the manner it is exactly programmed to act. The machine does not have enough complexity to act beyond its own programmatic design. A human, on the other hand, is so complex that we have the ability to go beyond our mechanistic existence. Love is an example of something beyond mechanistic existence and material reality. For this reason, love allows a human to unconditionally affirm existence, whether it be our own, another person's, or something else entirely.

This road,
This wonderful road,
We hope that by the end,
Wherever it leads,
It may be better than
Where it began.

For truth and the pursuit of happiness,
But happiness, by its nature,
Seeks to remain unchanged,
And truth has intrinsic failure,
Disproving itself from the moment it's declared.

For there are always
Other sides to the coin, unseen,
By seeking freedom
From the ambiguous and contradictory
Essence of being.

Only fools and knaves
Reduce happiness and truth
To their sole purpose and meaning.

A road deceptive, irrational, and non-repetitive,
This dangerous, precarious road,
Long drives forward with our burdens' load.
Hopefully, may we escape truth's tepid shabbiness.
Hopefully, may we move past a stagnant happiness.

Unconditionally affirming something is not within the scope of our genetic programming. It benefits us to have conditions. For example, if a friend betrays you, it is highly beneficial for you to stop being their friend so they cannot betray you again. In this scenario, your friendship is conditional upon your friend not betraying you. This is not love, but a friendship that exists by mutual benefit for both parties to serve life's goals and make life more convenient. This friendship is within the scope of our genetic programming. To keep the friendship and let the friend keep betraying you over and over is irrational and unreasonable. It will harm you in every way, so the only possible explanation for someone continuing such a relationship is love. For love exists outside of life; it does not care about the harm it causes, since harm only exists relative to life that has the intention of self-preservation. An entity with no intention of self-preservation cannot be harmed. For example, a rock can be destroyed, but you cannot harm a rock. Additionally, concepts like reason and rationality are firmly embedded in life. The term reason means: reasoning such that the logic benefits the reasoner. If reasoning did not benefit the reasoner, why reason at all? The point of reasoning is to make better decisions that benefit you; if they did not benefit you, it would be unreasonable. Life, when clashed against fundamental physical facts or to any sensible person, is intrinsically unreasonable. So, to continue living, one needs a tool that is beyond reason. Such a tool is love.

Virtue as its own reward, vice as its own pain,
Love is not for the herd, as love has nothing to gain
Those who seek love in hopes for value,
Move on from here. Your efforts are in vain.
Love is not for you. Love is not for the sane.

CONSCIOUSNESS AND LOVE

Very funny to me when others
mention magic as a bunch of little tricks.
For they know not magic
is the how we came about to exist.

The spiritual realm is not an esoteric theory. Spirituality emerges from the material realm's ability to exist in superpositions, amalgamating multiple states simultaneously. Spirituality from a modern perspective is the human sense of the infinitum of possibilities which can exist. When the universe is eternally expanding and contracting all possible states of existence have existed or will exist. It is just as equally possible that all the potential states exist at once since the eternal has no concept of time. The material realm then remains in a superposition of all possibilities or in a probability distribution of certain possibilities until it is observed, spirituality involves understanding the universe's undetermined state before it is perceived. It recognizes that the superpositionality intrinsic to the universe renders it undetermined before observation. When the mind perceives the superposition intrinsic to unobserved reality, it understands that the material realm is a hyper-condensation of the spiritual realm. In other words, the material realm represents the selection of one state from the superposition of states the universe held before observation.

When consciousness interfaces with the spiritual realm, it grasps that more physical states are possible beyond those already observed. When a person is more conscious from a deeper unconditional affirmation, and better performance of love, they condense the superposition of universes into something more real.

My love, the stars, they glisten so far.
The deep somber night does not hearken.
I am afraid we are alone in this apparition-splitting darkness.
The stage curtains open to entertain what, to me, is so foreign.
Our love is our test, the ultimate dance,
The ultimate performance.

Even though I have you to hold and to listen,
Why is it still that I suffer so deeply?
For it is in the gravest moments of my despair,
I refuse to expect anything fair, refuse to fall in disrepair,
You will never exist in truth, but only through my interpretation.
The truth, with or without your connection, is I remain in deep isolation.

My love, the stars, they glisten so far,
Yet what would they be without our perception?
The universe has created our inner light because it yearns to feel itself through us,
Existing as the burning white constellations, for them was simply not enough.

Their stronger consciousness reflects on them with a superior perception and cognition that then leads to a more pure and clear representation of reality. Consciousness, as the performance of constant self-affirmation through love, is the smashing of all the spirituality states into one state. Consciousness is the observation itself onto a wave function of probabilities of simultaneous states that collapses the wave into a particle-like definite state. Bringing the spiritual realm of superposition into the material realm of definite material reality. If reality and our universe is created by the self, then by expanding our consciousness we expand our reality. What else would the universe be but a trivial simulation without timid onlooking of a conscious mind.

When parents create a child they can care for the child through either their biological programming or through unconditional affirmation of the child through true love. If the child is cared for based on biological drives from the parents then parents will focus only on the biological necessities of the child and nothing more. This will likely lead to the child growing up feeling empty inside with all their material necessities fulfilled but never knowing deeper connections beyond the formalities of life. Just because a human is well fed, well educated, and socialized, does not make that human well loved, or make the human capable of self-loving. If a child is incapable of loving themselves they will not have a clear path to choosing continued existence unconditionally. If more children are raised with love more children will stay choosing life such that they live long lives, and experience consciousness fully. A life with all material necessities fulfilled and no love will lead to internal emptiness that will cause ambiguous indifference between continuing life or ending it. This downregulates the expansion of consciousness, which shows that love plays a mediating role in the expression of consciousness. A child on the other hand that is raised with unconditional love has a preference to continue their life because love makes existence and reality profoundly worthwhile. Existence doesn't have to be meaningful; it just has to be better than nothing for it to be worth selecting over nothing. A meaningless life with love is worth living over not existing at all. The more love a human receives the may not be related to how successful they are in terms material reality and life's purposes like money or power, but love beneficial to improving the psychological resiliency of a person. No matter how tough life gets the person will keep fighting because they have love embedded into their heart. However, if the child is raised devoid of love, they will find life meaningless purposeless and find it indifferent to choose between life and death. This causes more risk to permeate the child's life, as whenever the conditions become in inexpedient or torturous the indifference between existence and nonexistence can turn into a preference for nonexistence. In the end, finitude has its pride and eternity its self-sufficiency.

I live life for the moments that pass.
They adorn upon me with subtle charm,
in between the bells tolling my soul's alarms.
It is not that you are not enough for me,
but that there is not enough of you for me.
I need more of whatever you are.

Brick by brick to construct a life of beauty,
that knows volumes of pain and tragedy.
If love departs, they grieve—
life is too fascinating for me to ever leave.

The example of children who receive an education yet feel empty inside is commonly exemplified in inner-city public schools. Multiple factors contribute to this, ranging from trauma caused by overt violence to emotional neglect due to unstable home environments. Teachers in these schools often report that students have an overwhelming sense of doom, a belief that no matter the quality of education offered, any attempt will result in embarrassment or failure. This sense of hopelessness leads to high psychological distress, lower academic achievement, and elevated dropout rates. I remember hearing an inner-city teacher mention in an interview, "It's not that the kids don't want to learn; the problem is that they don't want to be alive at all." When a person is struggling with deep inner turmoil and is unsure whether they want to live or die, education can appear bland, meaningless, or trivial. In such circumstances, the need for emotional healing is far greater than any lesson plan. Moreover, beyond overt violence, post-industrial societies —especially those shaped by individualism—are often designed to cause emptiness and stress. Humans have evolved over hundreds of thousands of years to be accustomed to nature— trees, butterflies, starlit skies, and varied landscapes. Yet, we expect our children to love life when they are surrounded by nothing but concrete buildings and cars. Growing up without a sense of community and without nature in sight drains the charm out of life.

A child raised in such an unforgiving urban environment, combined with the absence of unconditional, self-affirming love, faces a maddened struggle of despair. The only way out would be to beat the odds and find access to their inner reservoirs of love. Yet, more often than not, drug abuse or crime becomes the default response to cope with these overwhelming circumstances. This is why it is imperative to educate children on the fundamental understanding of love and its mechanisms. If children can learn to love life and themselves, they will become more resilient against the dangers they face and more open to embracing education. One day, our public education system will teach children how to unconditionally affirm their existence. One day, our schools will show them how to tenderly dance with their emotions, rather than suppressing or rejecting them. For love is the reason we engage in the precarious and ambiguous art of life, what else is more important for us to educate our children about? Just as being extremely wealthy is meaningless without love, becoming educated is also pointless without learning to love life.

Evolution does not occur
From everyone acting by what will make the species sure.
Life spurs from singular individuals
Doing what they personally prefer,
And the other portion of this coin—
Many... many dying in failure.
Then why should you suffer
    From solitude,
When it is the white-capped wave
    From which all blessings are moved.

Our education system should teach not only academic subjects but also the importance of love—why it's essential for personal growth and why loving oneself makes one worthy of an education. Similarly, education itself must be recognized as worthy of effort and engagement. Every intellectual pursuit of substance in human history is a result of love. How can we expect young students to pursue higher goals and truths if they do not even have the internal tools to love being alive? Without love, education becomes just another task to endure, rather than an opportunity to grow. Some people do not understand the internal turmoil caused by a life without love because, for some, they are the very cause of it. These individuals live within the bounds of life's purposes, suffering little when love is absent. They crave life, not because they love it, but because it's inherent in their genetic programming. The hedonist and the philistine do not perceive existential indifference. For them, wanting to be alive is obvious because of the potential for future pleasure. However, this craving for life stems not from profound understanding but from ignorance. What is pleasure, but *la petite mort*—a small death? Pleasure serves as a means to escape life's challenges. When they are not pursuing or experiencing pleasure, the hedonist and philistine default to discomfort with life. They may believe they are in control, but in reality, they are merely expressing their death drive.

There is no fire in my soul
Better described by the dark forest floor
Those branches that spider, roots that pour,
The wooded thicket that makes one feel whole

Slowly engulfed in waves of darkened green
allows one to know what so often goes unseen,
a simple hug teaches the brutal firmness of the tree,
to desire roots and reject all that is free,
Makes other types of life seem mere stupidity,

A soul that does not know fire,
For the damp dreary weather,
Knows and grows life uninspired.
cool to touch yet oddly warm,
clear and distinct in nature and form,
It does not spread upon every chance,
And it is slow to move, slow to dance.

In this sense, the hedonist and philistine are more nihilistic than the person who understands life's ambiguity. Life's value is utterly shattered when one understands love because love exists outside the bounds of value—it is an unconditional affirmation of life, regardless of life's inherent value compared to death. Love does not negotiate or take prisoners.

When a person is overflowing with love, they choose each moment to be alive. They choose, in every moment, to be conscious. They reject suicide as resolutely as they reject excessive pleasure, because those pleasures represent lapses in conscious presence. Love offers a constant, unwavering commitment to life, even in the face of suffering. It is the antidote to existential despair and the foundation of true education.

Why is love not connected to pleasure? Because pleasure is not an end, but a material process. All the pleasure in the world, but if you are missing love then what was the point? All the joy in the world and if you are missing love what was the point? By defining love through pleasure and joy then morphine or other drugs would be a path to overflowing love, however experiencing morphine is an excellent example of how pleasure can exist without adding any love. The wise know that reality has layers upon layers of lies. Love as it does not come from material reality thus has layers upon layers of truth. What resiliency comes from controlling the internal fountains of love. A mother and father who love a child and unconditionally affirm them cause that child to grow up in a certain psychological health and wellness that reflects something of divinity. Love from the self; however, is what manufactures true divinity. Self-love is a more powerful and dangerous love. It shines like a sun and if one gets too close it can eviscerate flesh.

Conversation with a genie:
I ask, "Why do you let me wish for anything except love?"
Genie: "I am an illusionist. Money and power are illusions. Love is the only thing that truly exists. For that reason, I cannot change it."

There are metaphysical elements of love not captured by the historical usages of love in our natural languages. Specifically, the capacities for love to form self-causatively and self-referentially. While the objects and experiences we encounter in our everyday life have common sense causes; however, what causes love? Is it beauty, fascination, admiration? All these stated causes are derived from the purposes of life. Beauty is related to evolutionary fitness, and fascination or admiration are caused by an acknowledgement of positive performances. Love due to Proposition II is outside the bounds of life's purposes and thus cannot have a material cause. Love is the cause for itself. Love causes love, and it does not need an external cause, as it exists only in the spiritual realm. The second metaphysical aspect of love is its relation to the creation of reality. Everything in our reality is, in truth, unverifiable beyond our ego. Since the universe is projected within the mind, our experience of reality is entirely composed of the ego's projections. The accuracy of these projections is not guaranteed, and reality itself can be altered simply by changing the mind. Our reality is entirely dependent on our perception. Even in spiritual matters that lie beyond material perception, we still experience them through the mind reflecting upon itself. In many ways, consciousness is the mind holding a mirror up to itself. Expanding on the perception-dependency of reality: our reality is not its true existence but a mental simulation of it. Because of this, we can never truly know the world around us; we can only know our limited perception of it. Since our reality is shaped by us, we must continually affirm, moment by moment, that we want this reality to persist. When we no longer wish for it to exist, we have the power to change it—or to make it vanish entirely, potentially through madness or even suicide.

Tear out my eyes, and my tongue.
My gashes drip under the sun.
Blood pools below,
Life lets go.
Clean my ashes from the stov—
Still, always, will be left,
An overflowing lov—

The counterargument suggests that if one person perceives an aspect of reality and another independently perceives the same aspect, both can reasonably expect that what they have perceived exists beyond their individual perceptions. However, this argument overlooks the fact that perception is fundamentally driven by genetics and the sensory and cognitive organs of the body. If two humans share sufficient genetic overlap, their sensory organs—eyes, ears, brain, skin—will react similarly to the same stimuli or even produce similar hallucinations. In such cases, their independent perceptions of a phenomenon could stem from identical genetic activations rather than an external, objective reality. Even repeatable experiments conducted through formal empirical methods are intrinsically tied to human perception and constrained by its limitations. While empiricism provides powerful tools to sense, model, and predict reality, the results must ultimately be interpreted by human cognition and perception. Thus, no matter how compelling the evidence, we remain unable to definitively prove the existence of an objective reality. Empiricism cannot prove objective reality because proving it would require transforming the proof into something perceivable by human sensory organs. This transformation inherently reduces it to a perception, which cannot be verified as an accurate representation of objective reality. No matter how robust the evidence for objective physical laws that describe the universe, these laws are conceptualized and verified through human perception and cognition. As a result, it is impossible to know objective reality free from the filters of human perception and cognition. It is akin to creating a courtroom where the accused criminal is also the judge deciding whether the crime should be punished. We rely on perception and cognition to understand objective reality, while having nothing outside of them to do the understanding, and we expect to come to some truth beyond what perception and cognition are capable of.

The millennia's softly knock as seconds,
Warm are all the gods that beckon.

The world teems with ideas that shimmer and seduce, wrapping themselves around our minds like the velvet tendrils of some intoxicating dream. We speak their names in reverence, pledge ourselves to their service, and build monuments to their power. Yet, how many of these ideas exist beyond the fragile architecture of our belief? These constructs, these phantoms that haunt our thoughts, these are our spooks. The spooks with howl through the hallways, the juju up the mountain. They are the shadows we mistake for substance, the specters that command our devotion not through truth, but through the illusion of inevitability. Like whispers in the dark, they are terrifying until the light reveals their emptiness. To confront a spook is to wrestle with one's own enchantment and step, at last, into a clearer understanding of the world. Consider the state. It rises before us as a monolith, an indomitable presence to which we attach our allegiance, our identities, our very lives. We speak of the state as though it were a singular entity—an actor with intent, a hand that governs, a voice that commands. But what is this state if not the sum of countless human actions, incentives, and ambitions? It neither breathes nor wills; it neither speaks nor loves. It is a mirage conjured from the sweat and striving of individuals, whose disparate desires are cloaked in the fiction of unity. Yet we imbue this abstraction with agency, morality, and even the power to define the sacred. The state, like a god fashioned from clay, derives its authority not from its own being but from the worship we heap upon it.

Why so many problems, Evan?
For there is another mistress that drains
my fuel to seduce, and oh' does she love poetry,
The woman, who in conquering lust, lays claims,
to my soul, forever in perpetuity.
Every time I die, she returns to resuscitate me.
Who else can I love, but thee, oh eternity!

Do you feel its weight now, this illusion? It presses upon us because we believe in its form. We pledge our lives to defend it, offer our blood to preserve it, and bow our heads in submission to its laws. But step closer, peer into the fabric of this creation, and you will see it unravel into the actions of individuals: some greedy, some noble, most merely surviving. Where, then, is this mighty entity? Nowhere but in the collective dreams we have refused to question. The phantom that wraps itself so tightly around the human story? Skin darkened by sun, eyes shaped by winds, hair coiled or flowing—these are the markers we use to divide ourselves, to draw boundaries where none exist. Look closely, though, and you will find no genetic wall, no clear frontier separating one so-called race from another. Human diversity is a river, its tributaries mingling and merging until no beginning or end can be discerned. And yet, this illusion of separateness persists, etched into our histories and institutions, perpetuating the illusion of division.

They do not need philosophy!
They do not need poetry!
Until the void pulls them into
its infinite gripping pits of despair.
Then suddenly poetry
and philosophy are amazing!

Even life itself, both in classifications of sex and species, is not immune to superstition. Nature is a weaver of spectrums, a painter of infinite gradients. The chromosomal research exposes its arbitrariness of sex. We speak of species as though they were self-evident categories, distinct and unyielding. But nature's boundary is a mirage. Hybrid creatures, the flow of genes across supposed barriers, the continuity of evolution—all these reveal that life is not partitioned but fluid. The wolf does not become the dog in a single breath, nor does one species vanish into another without leaving behind echoes of connection. To insist on rigid taxonomy is to impose a grid upon the ocean. It may help us navigate, but it will never capture the boundless truth of life's interconnectedness.

Then, there is morality—the spook that reigns above all others, the whisper in the soul that demands we distinguish good from evil, right from wrong. The universe itself is silent on these matters; it spins in indifference, its stars unmoved by the struggles of humankind. Yet we, fragile and yearning, carve out moral codes and write them into stone, into scripture, into law. How often do we invoke gods to lend weight to our moralities, as though divinity itself might descend to sanction our desires? But if such a god exists, how could we presume to know its mind? Our moral systems are human constructs, born of culture and history, shaped by necessity and fear. Some argue that morality is essential, that without it, society would dissolve into chaos. However, the point of discussing the drawbacks of arbitrary moral prejudices is to take hold of it with clarity, to reshape it in service of life and flourishing, to let go of the illusions that make it a tool of oppression. To master it rather than to be enslaved by it. The spooks surround us, woven into our language, our thoughts, our very being. They create dissonance, bind us in contradictions, and make us feel betrayed by a world that does not conform to their promises. Yet to see them as they are—not real, but constructs—is to liberate ourselves. It is to step into the light, to accept the amoral dance of existence, and to live without fear of phantoms. What remains after the spooks dissolve? The world is raw and vivid. The river flows, the mountain rises, and the flesh warms beneath the sun. Life does not need illusions to justify itself and its internal beauty. It is enough to be, to breathe, to move on its own. Let the spooks fall away. Let us live unclouded, free to marvel at the vast, unyielding truth of existence itself.

In the Will to Life, rejecting suicide consistently affirms an organism's existence, we find that, through perception and cognition, an organism is self-hallucinating and self-producing its reality. When reality and life are self-created, and the self has the capacity to terminate its own cognition and perception through suicide, the affirmation and continuance of such perceptions and cognitions result from self-referencing and self-causing eternal love. Reality-causing love is the force that drives consciousness and the presence of mind within the represented reality. It is continually represented in the mind through the mind's eternal love for its self-conceived existence. These investigations suggest two possible extensions to the metaphysical conception of love: first, a love that causes itself, and second, a love that causes reality by being produced through consciousness, perception, and the cognition of the self and its unconditional, continual affirmation of existence.

So now tell me,
What would you represent
If you had nothing you loved to see?
What would you will if you did not love anything, really?
Without love, what person would you form yourself to be?
Why would the mind create the butterflies, the bees,
Or the little apples that fall from the trees?
If it did not come from love, birthed over and over, within?

Love birthed—recurrently, painfully,
Luridly and grotesquely.

Every moment we are conscious is an affirmation of an option in a *choice*, for there is always suicide as another selection to make. Every moment we are present or conscious, we are choosing to be so. If a choice is not made just being alive is not enough to be conscious. A person can be awake and performing normal actions while much time passes without realizing what they are doing, until they snap out of their trance-like state. This lapse of consciousness shows how we can navigate the ebbs and flows of life, functioning perfectly yet remaining unaware. The material world's interface with the spiritual world is consciousness. Defining consciousness is challenging from an empirical perspective, as empiricism is rooted in mechanistic conceptions of reality and often dismisses the spiritual. When a material organism acts and thinks beyond its genetic programming to serve life's purposes, it experiences consciousness. For example, when a world-class athlete performs optimally, they are not conscious of every muscle movement or the causes of their decisions. The athlete's consciousness is limited because they are focused on winning the competition, much like an organism focused on survival and reproduction. Both the athlete and the animal seeking survival operate mechanistically, in tune with the purposes of life. When an eagle is laser-focused on diving toward its prey, it acts based on muscle memory, not conscious thought. The eagle functions in synchronization with its biological programming, down to the genetic level. Another example is when a person experiences some flow state in which they are completely captivated by whatever they are doing, the body, mind, and perception are completely engaged during this state where a person is not aware of their own existence as a lapse of consciousness. Consciousness only exists when an organism has the privilege to think beyond its own advantage and programming. Humans, in increasing numbers, are achieving that privilege. The number of humans in the leisure economic class, which do not need to work, are increasing as the world develops more and more humans do not have to use their full strength to pursue the goals of life on the lowest orders of necessities for survival. Those humans with free time and underutilized strength can think beyond life, and experience consciousness. What lies beyond self-advantage exists beyond the material realm and necessitates the spiritual realm.

This oppressively beautiful world we share.
Taking from the same time, water, and air,
Turned my back on the glistening stars and heaven,
Has freed every facet of my loving expression,
Exalted for my eyes stay level and sharp in stare,
my hands and lips, forever, untainted with prayer.

Once there is a clear conception of how spirituality and love are connected to education and the whole of reality, we must ask: could this connection explain why humans are capable of so much more over other life forms? A human surpasses other organisms only because of our ability to conceptualize and transfer ideas to one another. These ideas are then used as tools to expand capabilities of a human to beyond what the physical body is capable. Civilization itself is an accumulation of thoughts and tools developed by past humans, particularly those related to agriculture, war, and God. Wherever civilization exists, we see temples dedicated to gods, highlands meeting lowlands, and rivers flowing into oceans. Highland pastoralists compel lowlanders into surplus-producing agriculture and use their privileges to occupy powerful clerical roles, which evolve into governments. But why does the concept of gods have a mysterious connection to civilization? God represents what is beyond the material and the physical. Without God as a metaphysical and linguistic tool, a leader could not convince others to do something outside of their material desires. For example, sharing resources with a stranger or risking one's life in a war are completely irrational from a biological perspective. Without a conception of what lies beyond the material, one becomes a slave to biology and the animal instincts. While love conveys what transcends material life, God provides an alternative way to communicate this idea. History demonstrates that God is a highly effective means of articulating the concept of the beyond and persuading people to act beyond their own biological interests. There are two types of godless individuals. The first type is the person who, after understanding the concept of God as communicated by others, chooses to reject it. The other is the person who has never fully grasped the idea of God due to inadequate exposure or understanding. Thus, atheists can be divided into "oblivious atheists," who are unaware of the concept of God altogether, and "rejecting atheists," who consciously reject it. Oblivious atheists, have no conception of anything beyond the material world, and what they physically perceive is all they understand to exist. Their actions align strictly with biological imperatives: eating when hungry, attacking when angry, and fleeing when frightened. These actions are driven by material self-interest. If a large group of people behaved purely according to biology, civilization could not form.

The graveness of gravity. How it curves me. How it pulls me. Pulls me with it.

Yes, mass is energy, and space, time, but could energy be the concentration of space. Energy be shaken waves upon its fabric? Reduce! Reduce! The empiricists taste, the empiricists only interest. With our caricatured neurons we can replicate a human! With our big bang we can find the secret to life! The secret that once we find will solve everything! All our problems!

The graveness of gravity. How it pulls me. Pulls me. Our world is the condensate of the spiritual. Time, we think a cone, but with one eye in the tube the other end always looks smaller.

Cooperation requires self-control and the willingness to perform tasks contrary to immediate desires. Many pivotal battles that shaped our current way of life were won by soldiers, for example Roman legionaries, who stood their ground and fought to the death, defying their instinct to flee. This discipline is connected to understanding what is beyond biology and is communicated using Gods as linguistic tools to do so. The example of a soldier committing to an action beyond the expediency of biological preference mirrors the need for most other roles in society to function with an understanding of action beyond oneself. A cleric without God will change the accounting unethically to benefit themselves. The agricultural laborer will only toil until they have cultivated enough for themselves not seeing a need to produce excess. Civilization is dependent on people thinking beyond their personal preferences dictated by biology. Attempting to communicate beyond the material requires either tedious metaphysics, or talking about "God's will," which is the easier option for a motivational speech before battle.

Where I am from, the pines grow upside down,
That noble tree,
ashamed now,
grows inwardly.
They now think that poetry,
comes from the mind's machinery.
They think now an education is an investment,
and should be analyzed by money spent.
When they reach the deepest, darkest despair,
they turn to the rope,
they turn to the chair.

'Tis not God that made man, but man who made God, says the belief held by the refined. Though, does that mean we should hate rather than love what we have designed? One day we will have civilizations built on the temples of love rather than the temples of gods. It is capitalism and industrialization—the concrete buildings and cars—that is the maturation of civilization by those who can think beyond themselves. These are the same people who know a lot about God, but not much about love. One day, men will unlearn worshiping another and instead learn to unconditionally affirm themselves. From following these proposed conceptions of God, morality and concepts such as "good" and "evil" is the intermeshing between material instincts and religious frameworks. Morality can be determined from mechanistic biology by discerning what is "good for the species" and "good in general," and what is "evil for the species" and thus "evil in general." Thus, an oblivious atheist can have a conception of morality without ever being introduced to the ideas of God, since they will have a natural understanding of what is good and bad for the people around them. A rejecting atheist is also capable of grasping what is good or bad for the people around them without believing in God. For this reason, people of completely independent and often opposing religious ideologies will have the same conception of good and evil actions or valuations, as it is an obvious representation of good being a reduction of harm. This is how pagans show similar actions of compassion and care throughout history when compared to the monotheists despite profoundly different conceptions of reality. Love, as it operates beyond the futility of limited biological processes, carves a path beyond the prejudices of valuating the world through good and evil, freeing us from a mechanistic utilitarian understanding. The concepts of good and evil are what ground peoples' conceptions of good to the material. Love however has no such prejudices. No such earthly ties.

Where I come from the pines grow upside down,
And the gods walk carelessly and unbound,
The gallows work without much sound,
And the bodies pile into mounds.
When you are close to me,
Materially,
Is when you are farthest,
For it is when my eyes can look into yours the clearest,
And I can finally glimpse into my true interest,
I am left disappointed you may be too far behind,
Your internal toil and disquiet are not the same as mine.

The way you act, socially mediated, unlike the buried truth that you are,
All these years and you have shown me less than a fleeting breath,
so, you wait to undress your inner wardrobe only after death?
For it is one day our finest will walk naked close and afar.

Every higher culture's beginning, almost a necessity, is violence as its precursor. Advancements in art, science, and governance always have their roots in conflict and cruelty. From the earliest points of written history, peoples from rugged lands developed the custom of invading and subjugating the original inhabitants of the new lands to which they arrived. From the Māori to the Aztec, to the Mongols, to the Ottomans, to the English, when we list great peoples, we are quick to forget the violence that was needed to achieve their goals. We forget that the ladders upon which they have climbed are made from bones and tied with sinew. The beginning of every civilization is a fight—a battle that is unequal, unfair, unknown, and, most of all, immoral. In fighting, there is madness, an immoral gamble. Shall we rejoice in this madness? Shall we affirm the gamble, or deny it?

INSIGHTS ON ART FROM A NOVEL LOVE

When you have nothing left?
When everything touched spoils?
When love is peering into death?
How do the plants grow?
Sun, water, airy soil.
Care and time. That is how.

The best artists are often plagued by doubt and insecurity about their work. To release the fruits of labor despite perceiving them as inadequate, and understanding its impending criticism is an act of courage fueled by the force of love. The harsh judgment of others, and the possibility of failure are intrinsic to the expression of love, and derivatively part of a person's artistic expression. When that failure comes, in the moments of solitude, who else will remain by your side but you? On dusky nights with tasteless food and a dim sky bearing down on your shoulders, the only love you can rely on is the love you give to yourself. Art is the culmination and eruption of love created from the self into the world. True art, exhibits the same properties from the love which it is derived: it is purposeless, valueless, and useless in the transactional sense. Yet it is also irreplaceable, unrepeatable, untradeable, and priceless. Art matures as something *unique*, an expression that cannot be replicated or commodified. People have commercialized art, but humans have also commercialized other humans. Does that take away from the pricelessness of human life? I can create a title contract for ownership of the sun and moon and sell it to someone as of writing this. Does that mean the buyer will truly own them? True art, just as a well-educated noble human can never be truly owned, and never have a price, just like the sun and the moon. The highly personalized experience of creation and destruction art representation is a rejection of all things spook.

Through this transformation, art becomes the materialization of love. It is the process by which the intangible becomes tangible. It stands as a testament to something beyond the basic mechanisms of survival. Art affirms the importance of expression, even when that expression serves no utilitarian purpose—when it does not contribute to self-preservation, material advantage, growth, reproduction, or the expansion of capability. True art does not contribute to power, convenience, or the practical functions that sustain or enhance life. Rather, art is a transcendent expression—free from the servitude of material purposes—and is born from a love that seeks no material reward or agenda. In works that blend the artistic and the useful, the whole may not qualify as art, but components of it may contain genuine artistry. For instance, consider an elegantly designed airplane. While its aesthetic appeal may resemble art, its primary purpose is to optimize performance, making its design subject to the material constraints of reality. The artistic elements within the airplane's design—the aspects that transcend utilitarian requirements—may be seen as art, but the functional aspects are engineering, not artistry. Art, unlike engineering, is not servile utility. Its only allegiance is to the love and truth from which it is born.

Can you see,
see my oceans and seas.
Can you breathe,
Breathe the breaths of my leaves.
Can you see,
see my oceans and seas.
Can you breathe,
Breathe the breaths of my leaves.

Religious art occupies a similar position to engineering. These works have components that are either utilitarian or genuine expressions of love. On one hand, it can be an expression unconditional faith by an artist. On the other hand, it can represent calculated marketing for the expansion of the religion or specific ideologies. The components of an artwork that have the intention of spreading religious influence or recruiting and converting new members becomes closely aligned with marketing and brand management. These works and their components often aim to increase the material or social power of the institution, much like a business creates advertising to improve its sales and expand its economic control. The Church uses its position of patronage to dictate elements that served its agenda—such as the realistic depictions of biblical narratives to validate its mythology. However, despite certain constraints by the Church's material goals, the artist's personal vision and love may still shine through. Michelangelo's creative passion and overflowing love of artistic expression are evident in the Sistine Chapel showing how love and religion can form components of a greater whole. Thus, religious works must be viewed as containing both unconditionally affirming and utilitarian components. The former are representations of true art that transcends material utility, while the latter is tied to institutional purpose and the practicalities of life.

*The producing artist is in
a constant state of pregnancy.
The art is birthed when IT is ready.*

True art, as the materialization of love, transcends the mechanisms of life. It cannot be subjugated to any practical agenda—religious, economic, or otherwise. Its essence resides in the spiritual, the eternal, and the unconditional. It is a pure overflow of love, existing solely for its own sake. An artist must love like being a parent, one must love all their creations equally and unconditionally. Just as we love all of our children exactly the same, we shall not be servile to the inequality of biology or enslaved to the world's reactions. What, after all, what affirms existence beyond the mechanical purposes of life? Love—love expressed without agenda or calculation. It is art that serves as proof of our consciousness, of our spirituality, because it shows that we are capable of thinking and producing beyond our material programming. If our art lacks beauty, we must still love it just the same, for true love is not contingent on perfection. If your heart does not overflow with love so intensely that creating art feels essential to your sanity, then you should not create art. Forcing yourself to create, without it bursting out of you can harm the soul—or worse, reduce the profound artistic act to mere task, a slavish imitation. Art cannot be manufactured through obligation or external demand. One should create only when the need to do so bursts forth from within, when it becomes as natural as breathing or crying.

The joy of writing,
Is worth the pain of reading it after.
Pain is the learning emotion,
It causes for silence and tranquility.

To try to force art is like a tree trying to will itself to bear fruit. The tree does not consciously strive to create fruit; it happens effortlessly, as a natural consequence of its maturity, readiness, and the right conditions. So too with art—it emerges when the artist is ripe with love, with experience, with the urge to express. Art captivates because it reveals the manifold expressions of love humanity is capable of producing. Each work illuminates the diversity of the human experience, showing us not just how others love, but how love itself transforms into form and color, sound and movement. The artworks that most purely embody love—those that are born from an unconditioned, overflowing heart—are the ones that captivate us most profoundly. They speak directly to the eternal and the divine, bypassing the material concerns of society. The greatest blessings for an artist is to be absolutely and radically true to oneself, move beyond the oppression of society's prejudices, and to liberate their vision from the narrow expectations of cultural norms and conventional thought. When art arises from such liberation, it is an uninhibited manifestation of love, untethered from judgment or purpose. By contrast, the artwork that is rooted in intellectual deduction or constrained by the need to provide social commentary, while perhaps valuable, tends to be less interesting. Such works serve a purpose, but they are chained down to the conditions of reality, and are not a true expression of unconditional love and affirmation.

Reposting on boards,
More versions and copies,
Volume ensures rewards,
Cheers from the crowd!
Hopefully lots of views!
When the attention dies down,
The crowd turns around,
When the poesy loses value,
They burn and trash it,
Like a crumpled tissue.

True art transcends reason and analysis; it exists because it must, and therein lies its power. In many ways, the type of art you choose to perform—whether painting, drawing, poetry, photography, literature, theater, or another form—becomes a love language. Each art form offers a profoundly different way to express your love and your affirmation of life. The act of creating art is an intimate conversation between yourself and existence, and the medium you choose reflects the way your soul speaks its truth. It is not about the love you wish to give others, but the love you discover within yourself, for yourself, and for life itself. Solitude is essential for the creation of art because it allows you to withdraw from the prejudiced influence of society. In solitude, you are freed from the expectations and conventions imposed by the world around you. This withdrawal is not an act of isolation but one of self-discovery. It is a sacred process in which you define love for yourself—not as something dictated by external forces, but as an internal truth. Solitude creates the space to explore how you wish to express the overflowing love within you, a love that no one else can define because it is yours alone. From this cultivated love, art is born, not as an effort but as an eruption, a natural and inevitable overflow of the heart. The philistine, however, has a confused and narrow conception of both art and love. The philistine walks through galleries with fascination only for the technical mastery of works that seem to offer some re-applicability to utilitarian goals. They are enraptured by art only when they perceive its technical skill as something that could be useful in a practical sense. When confronted with contemporary art, they scoff and find it valueless because it lacks extraordinary utilitarian skill. To them, if art is easily replicable, it commands no premium pricing economically. The philistine only sees art as merchant's affair.

Imagine a world where I loved less.

Well, you have imagined a lesser world.

Imagine a world where I have loved more,

is it not a world where I have received more?

Greed and pride hallowed once entered through love's doors.

In this narrow sense, the philistine is correct—true art is indeed useless. It does not serve a purpose in the material world, just as a master is useless to the economy compared to a slave. While the slave is purposeful producing valuable goods and services, the master is usually relatively useless, and so it is with art. The philistine may replicate art through skill but will never create art born of love. Their disdain for true art arises because their spirituality does not extend beyond the material. They know how to reproduce but lack the ability to originate. To them, art that cannot be commodified is nonsensical, and thus they fail to understand that true art is an expression of consciousness, an outpouring of spirituality into creation. The philistine's error lies in their inability to see beyond the practical; they mistake the absence of utility for worthlessness, when in fact it is the absence of utility that gives art its transcendence.

Equally flawed is the person who believes beauty is the defining marker of great art. Beauty is servile to life; it is tied to attractiveness, health, and the instinctive desire for integration and expansion. Beauty has a purpose—it is a mechanism of life—and as such, it cannot define art as the manifestation of love. Love, unlike beauty, is indiscriminate. It knows no conditions, no hierarchies, no qualifications. Great art is birthed in unconditional affirmation, not in the pursuit of beauty. To criticize art for lacking beauty is to misunderstand its nature entirely. Such criticism assumes that art exists to serve life, to attract, to elevate—but love, which is the essence of true art, is free from all these purposes. Art does not seek to expand the self; it seeks only to affirm existence as it is. It transcends the mechanisms of life, offering no utility, no purpose, no service. Its value lies in its uselessness, in its ability to express love that is pure, unconditional, and eternal. When we approach art with this understanding, we see it not as an object to be judged or utilized but as a manifestation of the boundless, purposeless love that defines our humanity

I know a little secret about life,
I know a little secret about life—
a sad secret that nobody wants to know.
I can shout it from the mountains, put it in the speakers,
and despite its truth, no one will believe or repeat it:
that the losers of life are the ones who end up winning.
Or, better put, the ones who end up remaining.
They hold life's tender wings with rough, insatiable mediocrity.
The winners end up killing each other too quickly
or die as childless artists.

This raises a profound question: if love is the foundation of unconditional affirmation, how can so many brilliant artists end their lives in such tragic ways, through suicide or drug overdose? Their art, often regarded as a manifestation of love, seems to contradict their untimely deaths. The answer lies in the fact that many of these genius artists have not fully matured—either intellectually or emotionally—by the time they reach the pinnacle of success. They have not cultivated a deep, unconditional love for themselves, and their affirmation of life remains dependent on external circumstances. When faced with challenges such as romantic rejection, betrayal, or the many painful events life can bring, their self-worth and self-love falter. Instead of drawing strength from an internal well of love that remains steadfast in the face of adversity, they allow external events to define their value. In such moments, rather than feeling empowered to affirm and love life, they may instead be overwhelmed by the thought that death might offer an escape from their suffering. They have not nurtured an internal fountain of love that can sustain them through life's inevitable trials, and thus crave death.

To be less than yourself,
    Less than the ocean... less than the sea,
      is <u>slavery.</u>
Honey, can you see my burdens, see my swaying sea,
serious texts may offer gravity,
change everything with their outlook,
but to some lesser degree,
There is a part of becoming
that is learning,
what can never be in a book.

To understand this, imagine a cup filled with water, where the water represents love. The artist whose cup is brimming, spilling over the sides, represents a healthy, mature, and full artist. This is someone who not only loves themselves unconditionally but whose love overflows into their art and interactions with the world. The full cup represents the artist who has found self-love and unconditional acceptance, allowing their love to spill into their creations, becoming a channel for deeper self-expression. The cracked cup, however, constantly loses water. The artist with a cup that has a crack at the bottom, leaking water slowly, symbolizes the talented but fractured artist. These artists create their work not from an overflow of love, but by draining what little they have left inside. They possess some love, but it is constantly being depleted. The artist whose cup is completely empty—without any water or love inside—represents those who, despite their talent and consistent creation of profoundly deep art, lack the self-love necessary to maintain internal peace, mental health, and joy as their life becomes more fragile. The act of creating art, rather than being an expression of overflow, becomes an exhausting drain that diminishes their will to live. They pour their love into their art, but the act of creation comes at a cost, as they continually deplete their internal reservoir. When the love no longer flows freely, they turn to drugs to force more water into their cup. Eventually, even their reserves of love run dry, and with no internal source of affirmation or peace left, suicide becomes the only escape from their internal turmoil. This battle of internal conflict often leads to a fragile mental state, where their work becomes a form of self-exploitation, an unsustainable process that inevitably takes its toll.

People talk so much about God this God that,
What do they know of God?
No more than the next howling monkey.
The priest too, begs at the worker bees for honey.

This dynamic is invisible to the observer. The artist who is draining themselves of love to produce art may create work that is as powerful and compelling as that of the artist whose cup is overflowing. To the outside world, there is no distinction between the two. Both may produce extraordinary art, but the artist with the cracked cup is dying inside, while the artist with the overflowing cup is thriving. When your cup of self-love is full, your art naturally overflows from the abundance. In contrast, artists who have not yet discovered unconditional, overflowing self-love often force their art into existence by cracking the cup or tipping it over, ultimately draining it of love. This kind of art can be thought of as a "love debt."

After Basquiat became rich and famous, he started using heroin. He found that his art sales were slowing down, and he was growing less popular with critics. Basquiat noticed that his paintings made while on heroin were more popular and sold better, but when he painted sober, his work received more criticism for being stale. By taking heroin, both Basquiat and Cobain were cracking their cups to force the water and love out. The sober artist cannot endure the pain of cracking their own glass of love, but the drugged artist can, for the heroin numbs the pain. They made a deal with Bacchus, a more dangerous deal than Mephistopheles.

Beautiful is the word for the poets who leave their work unsigned:
A beauty I have not yet attained.
I sign my work from part selfishness part voluptuousness.
Of which, I am not ashamed.

Unable to fill their glass with self-love, they became concerned with what critics said about their art, and with how it sold. The full, overflowing artist swats away critics and customers like pesky flies. But Basquiat's love eventually ran dry from the spillage, and as his love emptied, so did his affirmation of life. He left us impoverished; another beautiful soul lost. The famous, genuine artist does far worse than sell their soul to the devil. The devil is evil, yes, but he is not a beast or monster—he too is born from eternal love. Worse than a prostitute who sells their material body, the famous artist sells their most valuable possession: the dynamism and eternal radiance of their tender heart. And who does this famous artist choose to sell their possession to? Not the devil! Far worse: to the squabbling rabble. The canaille, forever starved of love, survives only by exploiting fleeting luck and the insolent abuse of others' goodwill. Their shallow valuations and insatiable hunger feast on the artist's soul, draining it until they are left a hollow, empty carcass—torn limb from limb, with nothing left, even for scavengers.

INVESTIGATING ÉRŌS

Romantic love does not know of eternity. It knows well time.
Wherever love and sex are intermeshed, aligned
How much are you truly present?
Or rather, it is an escape into transience?

They are everywhere. In the floorboards, behind the fences! And they sit around without much urgency. They know they can keep moving forward, and they are unafraid of the future to which they are fated. They are passive, for they know victory is not achieved by activity. They can take as much time as they need, for they know their test is of love, which is unbounded by time. They think our love is weak. They think we are unaware of its little secrets. Look at the way they revere the endurance of pain. Endurance, absorption of pain—that is what stands them above the rest. The ability to endure. Marathons are inadequate metaphors for lifetimes. Lifetimes are rich and complex. They require a different endurance. My right hand grows heavy from its armament against this ignorance. Lo, my brothers, lo!

Érōs, you pestilent god. Out of your anger and confusion over my unusualness, you have stuck so many arrows in me that now I am immune! As if now, I am vaccinated. You thought I couldn't find rationality in your induced madness! But I did. You made me think I would never recover but look at me now!

Look at the health now. My love bubbles and foams upon fine-sanded shores, and the sound of its gentle waves soothes the most blessed to sleep. You have cut my work out for me! In your millennium-long conniving manipulation, you have come around to dominate our understanding of love. You found a way to reduce our common understanding of love to just you. Now they succumb even to suicide when their desire for your misconstrued love is unfulfilled. Soon my work will mature love to beyond what is induced by some armed and blind flying child!

She goes on unscrupulous, careless,
Questionability surrounds her every choice in dress,
And for herself she so rarely knows what's best,
Though tis not her treasures hath won my interest,
For What brings abrupt ends to my poking jests,
To forever turn my focus into love's gentle caress,
Is whatever causes the beating in her little chest.

Where love is absent, I see everywhere the desire for suicide. Why? No life affirmation, no self-affirmation intrinsic to the definition of true love. One cannot look beyond the romantic if one does not have words, if one does not *have poetry* that goes beyond. Beyond the puddle of romantic love is an ocean with depths unknowable by merely investigating the surface. Evaporating and condensing such water yields something drinkable to help a person survive when love's dehydration approaches death. If the process is perfected and industrialized, it will yield an abundance, making future generations unable to understand that the scarcity ever existed. I am referring here to the ocean of self-love.

Can there be erotic love that is true love? In summary, no, and neither should there be! Eroticism and romantic pursuits should be performed based on your attraction to another person and the viability of maintaining a healthy relationship with them. Thus, the erotic and romantic are firmly derived from Proposition I of life and its purposes. Eroticism is rooted in the material, and we should keep it that way, as it is not enhanced in any way by Proposition II true love. True love can only emerge once the relationship begins maturing into something more than simple sex. It is the same distinction between love in engineering and love in religious art, where it is necessary to decompose the ideas into simpler parts that can then be more easily identified as love or not love. The components of an erotic relationship that are unconditionally affirming of the partner constitute true love.

Shrapnel strew.
We move,
separately now,
think you?

Meanwhile, the components of a relationship, such as the reasons for being attracted to someone are often rooted in biological benefits servile to utility and life's purposes, which do not constitute true love. Even loving someone for their personality, if it stems from their possessing traits likely to result in material success or life-related advantages, falls short of true love. People with good personalities might make better professionals, spouses, or parents—attributes beneficial to the material realm and thus a conditional affirmation. You affirm that the partner is attractive based on conditions such as having a symmetrical face and body or a personality suited to professional or parental roles. Since this relationship is conditional, it is not true love.

And blood washes away in the rain.
Tears hide in the cloudy grey.
No sun shines upon the grain,
for I may never see you again.

There can still exist components in a romantic relationship that are unconditionally affirming. For example, a person who is dating another can still want to be with them even if they face failure or fall ill. That component of the relationship is true unconditional love. However, if the relationship was initiated from mutual attraction, then the relationship as a whole is not true love but a mixture of eroticism and love. Unconditional true love, as derived from Proposition II, would render all good and bad qualities irrelevant to your desire and affirmation of the person. True love also appears possible regardless of the duration of a relationship. I have not seen any viable argument that the length of a relationship impacts the perfection of love expressed or the quality of the relationship. True love is not inherently required to last a lifetime. Love that exists from age 20 to death at 80 is temporal and limited just like a shorter love period of less than five years is temporal and limited. From the perspective of eternal love, they are the equivalent—especially considering that each moment in true love is eternal. Eternal love resonates and echoes throughout the universe.

Diamonds,
Shining brilliantly.
And pearls,
I hear, glisten too.
Carelessly, I throw those
rocks back to the dirt.
When in my arms,
I could have you.

True love found in erotic contexts is oxymoronic. When one is having an erotic experience, it is thoroughly attached to life, as sexual selection is firmly purposeful in improving the health of a species intergenerationally. To have true love in a sexual context would require ignoring the health, character, and physical attributes of the partner—an act that would diminish attraction, would it not? This defeats the purposes of biological sexual selection. Erotic love, which under deeper scrutiny will always lead to some evolutionarily advantageous attribute as its cause, is a gamble. What else is to be expected from a blind child shooting arrows? One person gives another everything without any obligation for reciprocation, leaving them vulnerable to mortal wounding. This game of love is merely a prisoner's dilemma. So how does one win? Through reciprocation, copying, and matching. To put it plainly: wait for someone to be madly in love with you, then love them back with absolute certainty. Let their under-education leave them vulnerable and use that vulnerability as an opportunity to demonstrate your trustworthiness. Turn Cupid's arrows into a tool for yourself, master them, and avoid their seductive slavery. What if you feel as if nobody will fall madly in love with you? Then turn yourself into someone worth falling madly in love with. You have enough time and not enough excuses. To eternal self-love, the idea of changing oneself is an absurdity—as if you did not deserve self-love to begin with. However, perhaps the process of changing oneself into someone worthy of love is, in itself, an act of self-love.

In your love, I found a thousand truths,
It nullifies the learnings of any school.

Additionally, restraining your love in an erotic relationship is always highly advantageous. Harvest the hydroelectric energy from the stream instead of bursting open the dam. Restrained love is more desirable to the other person in the relationship. It shows the partner that you are not willing to fall in love with just anyone and that you need time to develop your feelings. If it takes time to grow into love, it means the person learned things about you along the way that made them feel love for you. In other words, their love is not indiscriminately applied to anyone crossing their path (Agápē). Instead, it is personalized and directed toward you because their heart sees you as special. A possible strategy is utilizing Érōs as bait to turn a romantic relationship into Storgē. Perhaps ludic love can serve as the bait to later transform into that good, reliable Storgē. Storgē is always favorable because it is a less impassioned love with a duller flame—it lasts longer and is harder to extinguish. It is a more robust, safer love that assures both partners their love will not vanish if they become ugly or sick. Érōs, on the other hand, offers no guarantee that love will endure once a partner becomes unattractive or ill.

I love you like the solemnly looming blue night sky. I love you like wet footsteps over cobblestones from shady passersby. I love you like the gentle croon of a mother's lullaby.
I love you like the breeze flowing over the dozing trees, bristling leaves in the cool night air. Many times silenced and impaired, yet it still whispers — everywhere. All the little loving looks and moments thoughtlessly shared are now entrapped in eternity's celestial snares.

Similarly, you rarely want to be with an Agápē lover because their love is universal and lacks discrimination. They have no reason to prioritize you over everything else in the universe.

Their love, applied equally and indiscriminately, will move on to the next person or object of attention. This is a wonderfully beautiful experience for them, but how does it benefit you? Why devote resources to a romantic relationship with someone who loves so indiscriminately?

On this topic, I must ask myself: is this subject worthy of my energy? The erotic and romantic, when misunderstood, can cause great pain to an unlearned person. The well-learned person, always flush with self-love, will never take intemperate action due to romantic betrayal or rejection. So why should I waste my time understanding romance when all I need to do is speak of the fountains of self-love? Equally, the problems emerging from the romantic can all be solved with basic education. Core tools like communication, psychology, and a proficient understanding of the profound neurological and emotional diversity among humans are always helpful. For example, consider something as simple as jealousy: some people believe that if a person is not jealous of their partner talking to someone else, then that person must not truly care about their partner. Others, however, view jealousy as an immature emotion, unbefitting a partner secure in themselves. Both conceptions of romantic relationships are matters of taste, but understanding the diversity of these perspectives equips one to handle situations more effectively as they arise in real life.

Material life is once again reduced to a matter of taste... as it so often is. For that reason, an erotic lover who values physical beauty is equal to a lover who cares only for character and soulfulness. Neither is greater than the other, as both affirm life! Friendship is an essential aspect of erotic love. It informs the selection process for choosing a partner, reducing the subjectivity and ambiguity inherent in the process. Philia is the black pepper, and Storgē is the salt, seasoning all erotic endeavors. To clarify, when discussing a mixture of Storgē and

Érōs, it refers primarily to a marriage where both partners are technically family under consummation and love each other as family. Marriage, in the most traditional sense, signifies the intertwining of Érōs and Storgē. Can true love be experienced with an immoral lover? Absolutely. However, the immoral lover will likely cause emotional harm and be generally dysfunctional —like a father who spends the day's wages on alcohol instead of clothing and feeding his children. In a marriage, an immoral lover will likely cause divorce unless their partner is equally immoral, which would likely lead to either escalating conflict or mutual acceptance of each other's nature.

Take my love,
Or the next!
It makes no difference,
So we need not fret.
I moved on, not from
Lack thereof,
But my commitments.

Take my love, and
You will learn:
The arts have always
Been above
The rank you've earned.

You can birth;
What can I create?
Tend to the hearth—
A family
I can not dictate.

My despair,
The most unusual of fates,
Necessitates a deeper love,
A stronger faith.

No longer do I covet or wait,
But knock down and press,
Into the most sacred blessedness—
Those eternal gates.

A lover is different from a sexual partner. When choosing a sexual partner, Prâgma seems to be the wisest path. A lover, on the other hand, can be found in any person, even a friend, as it requires only unconditional care and affirmation. A sexual partner or marriage serves life's material endeavors and is thus purely advantage-seeking. If love is shared between two sexual partners, such love is independent of the sexual nature of the relationship. Romantic love can be defined simply as being emotionally impacted by another person in a positive way over a significant amount of time. This positive emotion, however, can be outcompeted by a stronger positive emotion. Many people sacrifice a romantic partner to pursue their dreams because the pursuit and potential realization of a reality where those dreams come true provides more joy than romantic love.

And I wish I could tell you it was love,
But why leave our hearts a discourteous smudge?
It did not tremble my arms or touch—
For there was a gentle evil you sensed in such.

Memories, above all, are what I cannot bear.
I cherished most the stories we shared.
And that light, which constantly laughs, plays, and sings—
You are the universe that made me dare,
Dare to clip my wings.

My taste? Like in all things in Proposition I related to life, my taste in romantics is cold and cruel, a befitting match for my unscrupulous adversaries. First work toward material beauty. That is the strength of your army in these erotic wars. The next factor is strategic positioning. Just as you position your armies upon the hills, with scouting parties ahead, heavy infantry guarding resource caravans, and cavalry spaced for mobility, one must position correctly to win. A location with alcohol is no place to find a woman, nor is any place of excess or indulgence. She must be sober when you meet her. In her sobriety, you must see the attraction in her eyes at the moment of "hello." If there is no brightness in her eyes upon your appearance, be polite and move on. Never chase—that is as ludicrous as chasing a fish with your hook. However, if her eyes express something, your demeanor should reflect her interest back onto herself. She must see herself in you. Ask questions. Talk as if you are trying to find the inner workings of a clock without the ability to take it apart. How do you turn? Mechanical, quartz, digital? What gear ratios? hand design? Escapement? Winding mechanism? A good question can be more pleasant and rewarding than any expensive gift. Feel her energy and take your own emotions seriously. Let your unconscious mind do its intractable processing, find what feels right, and allow yourself to be irrational in affirming your emotions. It will be obvious when it arrives.

Never love in the romantic world. It's like loving war. A man who loves war comes across as ignorant and off-putting. War must be waged only when necessary. Erotic relationships should be engaged only when necessary—when the heart needs it. Higher romantics have no room for Proposition II defined love. Romantics are a celebration of the material—forms, linguistic expressions, actions, emotions. Not to be confused with true love. True love arrives to fill what is left when the material is degrading. Let the void materiality leaves within the erotic be filled with love as the opportunity arises. As material transforms into the eternal, those who look for love in a romantic partner immediately are rejecting materiality—

a negation of life. That is no marking of a higher soul. When you have her, that is when you have the proper soil to plant the seeds of love. Why do we work? To decrease the stress of our family. Her stress is carried epigenetically to our children. So, she needs to be without it. Children need to grow unclouded, clear in cognition. Their bodies will not be stunted. They will be fed quality food—food that makes you forget you ate it. Their clothing shall be made of natural fibers: cotton, wool, and hemp. Our cars shall be run-down. Our houses, architected to reflect our personalities, shall be spacious and located where mountains, rivers, and oceans meet. Where fresh air and cooling breeze have a consistent movement. Our children will own no toys, keeping their imaginations focused on the plants, animals, and stars, the toys of gods. Books and art shall fill our walls—not forgetting to include our OWN art, our OWN books. Many fall when they neglect the foundations. They don't understand the man that takes triple the time to erect his walls. They are confused by the foundation builders, thinking they are irrelevant to the actual house. My grounded piles run deep just as my callused soul. The lime clasts and volcanic ash of my concrete self-healed its gaps and cracks. Just as my once-porous heart has.

RELATING TO PHILIA

If the poem is shorter,
The higher the likelihood I will read.
For a short witty scribble.
I am weak willed, impressionable,
Impulsive, the most insufferable breed.

A friendship is a more precarious relationship than most would care to admit. Unlike familial bonds or romantic entanglements, there is little in the way of material or social necessity holding you and your friend together. The best friendships, paradoxically, are those that exist without reason, thriving purely on the joy of each other's company. In a romantic relationship, physical pleasure often serves as a gravitational force, binding two people even when their emotional compatibility falters. Blood ties, on the other hand, are fortified by the cultural and social pressures of family obligation, often masking the absence of genuine rapport. Friendship, by contrast, stands on a precipice; it requires no such crutch. It floats, untethered by external forces, and in doing so, it moves beyond the material into the spiritual. It becomes synchronized with the rhythm of perfect love.
Philia is not only the love entrenched in pure friendship, but also the general love of things or actions —a passion that transcends interest and becomes an essential element of life itself. To love what you do is to possess a guiding star, a force that shapes the direction of your days and defines the spirit with which

you move through the world. This form of love, if embraced fully, renders regret an impossibility. Consider the impoverished guitar player, wandering from bar to bar, offering his music for a modest wage. His life is a stark contrast to the famed musicians who play sold-out arenas and bask in luxury. Yet the guitar player is no less fulfilled, for his love of the instrument is so profound that he cannot bear to do anything else. It is not a lack of skill or opportunity that keeps him bound to his craft—it is the visceral, unshakable truth that anything else would feel like a betrayal of his soul.

I thought I alone burned my poetry, but 'tis not me doing the burning!
A phoenix lurks around these skies and rebirths the same souls in disguise!
One is condemned to experience everything again, in all manners, in infinite returning!
Take each morning, watch the sun rising, and realize the gold that litters the horizon.
There are many daybreaks deserving of dance. However, this one is of most importance.

In this way, the unsuccessful guitar player embodies the ideal life worth living. What value is there in comfort, in good food and shelter, in disposable income, if your days are not consumed by something you adore? Accumulate wealth, and then what? You will spend it on things you love? But spending is the act of a consumer, not a creator. Creation, that fiery act of bringing something into existence from the depths of your being, is the essence of life itself. To live without it is to suffer a kind of spiritual castration. The priest may know out of curiosity, the warrior may destroy with ambition, but only the poet creates with love. So why would anyone make money? The argument often goes that you must first do what you do not love in order to gather resources, which can then fund your true passions. Painters must buy paint and canvases; musicians must purchase instruments. This reasoning is logical, but love and art are not born of logic. They arise from a realm far beyond reason. The conqueror who marches into battle with meager resources does not rely solely on his material advantage. There is strategy, cunning, and craftiness needed when faced against the impossible. To be a conqueror one must know how to accept the real possibility of death. In the same capacity, if you want to do something you love, why should we accept any lesser philosophy than that of a conqueror? Love does not wait for the perfect conditions. It thrives in the face of adversity, flourishes despite the odds, and dares us to choose it with the ferocity of warriors and the tenderness of poets.

I can give you some new technology,
But will the increase in your power,
Or whatever new capability,
Do anything to stitch your heart back together?
For that can only be done with poetry.
The newest lucrative business offer
Is so fleeting and temporal,
When what I have to give is grave and eternal.

As a child, I remember the stifling monotony of sitting in the classroom, where the minutes dragged and the lessons seemed to suffocate under the rigid structure of scheduled time. Each subject, regardless of its complexity or simplicity, was confined to an identical period, as if learning could be measured by the clock rather than by understanding. The lessons that demanded more depth and exploration were cut short, leaving questions unanswered, while those that needed but a fraction of the time stretched unbearably, leaving us idle and restless. It was during these long, inert hours that I first felt the claustrophobic weight of time wasted, a dull ache that gnawed at my spirit. Yet when the bell rang, signaling recess, it was as if my soul was unshackled. The world opened up in those fleeting moments of play. Time would pass in an instant, so swift it felt almost cruel to be transported back into the dreary classroom. That feeling—when time disappears in the joy of doing—must be what it means to truly love something. The responsible and honorable pursuit in life, then, is to find that which makes time vanish in the same way it did in the rapture of childhood play. To discover work or a purpose that captures you so wholly that the hours slip through your fingers unnoticed is to engage in a true performance of love. This idea echoes Buddhist philosophies, which suggest that such immersion—this experiential acceleration of time—can separate the soul from suffering. It creates a hygienic, almost transcendent relationship with the cycle of life, allowing one to engage with existence in a way that feels light and unburdened, like the cleansing touch of a fresh breeze.

Owning nothing but dirt on my feet
The ground is where I choose to sleep
flowing joy as time ebbs and passes
Running free through the plains and grasses
A servant serving servants, asses working mules,
A self-made owner. A self-made fool.

To uncover this kind of love for work or purpose requires a deliberate withdrawal from the cacophony of external influences. For me, it begins with solitude. I step away from the incessant demands and expectations of others, retreating into the quiet spaces where my thoughts can roam freely. For weeks, sometimes months, I make no plans. I let my weekends stretch out like an open field, undefined and unclaimed. On those Saturdays, I wake without an agenda and ask myself a simple question: what do I want to do today? And then I follow that impulse, no matter how trivial or unconventional it may seem. Over time, patterns emerge. Week after week, if I find myself returning to the same activity, if it continues to spark joy or fascination, I begin to understand that I love it. This process, while healing and clarifying, is imperfect. It leaves me vulnerable to the whims of passing passions, the fickle tides of emotion. And so, I wonder: Can anyone truly master what they love? Is it even possible to wield control over such a profound and instinctual force? I do not know. I suspect not. Love, especially love for what we do, resists domination. It is a wild, untamable thing. Yet even in its unpredictability, the process of following it—of surrendering to it—has made me happier, healthier, and more alive. What worked for me may not work for you, for the path to discovering love is as unique as the soul undertaking the journey. Perhaps the only universal truth here is that the search is worth it, however you go about it.

And why is it that, when we look closely, we find that kings are no wiser or more exceptional than any other kind? It is because the gods measure our hearts, not our minds.
And what is it that forms the essence, the true substance, of our hearts? The answer is something every person already knows in part.

Love, when it manifests in action, carries inherent risk. To throw yourself into something, anything, is to risk failure. There are endeavors that are intrinsically valuable, like the unselfconscious play of a child, where the act itself is its own reward. There are others where the love stems partly from external rewards—material gain, recognition, or success. Imagine someone who loves computers, who spends their days assembling and selling them. If their love is tied to the profit of those sales, then it is not the computers they love but the money they generate. True love for an action transcends expediency; it is untethered from the material outcomes of the work. A person who genuinely loves selling computers will continue to do so even when it is not profitable, simply for the joy of the craft. And if they cannot, for practical reasons, they will wait patiently for the next opportunity, their passion undiminished. This distinction reveals the shallow nature of material attachments. Consider the love of money: those who claim to love it are, in truth, devoted to the things money can buy—food, shelter, luxury, convenience. Should money lose its value, as in times of extreme inflation, their "love" would simply shift to bartering or some other means of acquiring goods. This is not love but a utilitarian relationship with resources. True love, by contrast, does not pivot or adapt to convenience. It is steadfast and self-sufficient in the act itself. To love in this way is to transcend the transactional, to affirm unconditionally the worth of what you do, and to align yourself with the deeper rhythms of existence.

People often choose winding paths to finally get to what they love, but only pursuing love directly is higher performance of life, or honorable. Indirect paths always lead to remorse or regret. *Tamerlane built his kingdom part by part, kept it whole and strong, but all he had ruled over and won was worthless to his broken heart.* If you do become excessively wealthy, then what? What would you do with your time? Many find a sense of uselessness, purposelessness, and subtle dread after finishing a career that occupied all their time. Becoming so accustomed to the discipline of chasing success, they never learned to truly live for themselves, and are confused when they fall back to true ambiguous reality. The well-adjusted and educated may turn to helping their community, devoting yourself to a meaningful side project, or exploring pursuits you had always postponed. Yet, whatever path you choose, it would ultimately be guided by a species of love whether consciously or unconsciously. For instance, suppose you declare that your greatest love is for your community. Upon reflection, a significant part of that love likely stems from how the community nurtures and supports you. They may listen to you, spend time with you, or affirm your value. Or perhaps you've in theory absorbed the idea, from books or teachings, that valuing your community is a noble and virtuous pursuit.

A hundred lashings every day
Upon mine soul doth fall,
A hundred reconciliations by night
Healeth wounds withal.
having so much to mourn,
Forgiveness eludes my sight,
A hundred overcomings by morn,
To harden strength and might,
For pain deserveth naught, but
simple contempt and scorn.

People often deny these reasons, asserting their love for the community as selfless or pure. Yet, consider this: if a community mistreats someone, excludes them from its events, offers no support or warmth, how likely is it that the individual will continue to love that community? Our love for the community is often a reflection of self-love—a recognition of how the community uplifts and fulfills us. In return, we support the community because we know it will uplift others as it does us, creating a virtuous cycle of care, connection, and mutual reflection. This dynamic showcases the remarkable, though often unconscious, human ability to think theoretically about life and instinctively seek advantage within it. Because many people struggle to consciously articulate these theoretical frameworks, humanity has devised religions to translate such abstract principles into accessible narratives. The concept of gods personifies these ideals, offering a clear and compelling reason to extend love beyond oneself. Without such frameworks, the average person might struggle to understand why they should love another who does not directly benefit them, such as a stranger, or even why they should love parents and siblings who may not always reciprocate their care. This is likely why human civilization and the idea of god are so deeply entwined; these beliefs offer a moral architecture that bridges the self and the other, ensuring the continuity of shared love and responsibility.

Facing solitudes icy breath
Distant times since I have known
A soul capable to quell my stress
All the bitter remedies to detest,
the many tender nights shown
I've only ever grown -- facing everything alone,
I need not more time to mourn or de-stress
Lest caught in common moment of weakness,
Devastation my price for muted tones,
Love was all I found from the burned mess.

This reflective dynamic of love underscores the critical importance of self-love. The stronger and deeper the love you have for yourself, the more powerful its reflection upon the world becomes, like a beam of light intensified as it refracts through a prism. At its core, self-love is not mere vanity or selfishness; it is the affirmation of your own conscious existence. Before you can truly affirm the existence of another, you must first affirm your own being. Only through this foundational affirmation can you build the layered abstractions of love and purpose that allow you to connect with others and engage meaningfully with life.

When you love doing something—be it a profession, a passion, or a purpose—you are often operating at a higher layer of abstraction, built upon these underlying affirmations. At the most fundamental level, what you truly love is yourself, and from there, the people around you. From these origins, your love radiates outward, gaining complexity and depth as it reflects back upon the objects and actions you choose to dedicate yourself to. This capacity to abstract our love enables us to function within the intricate frameworks of modern society, turning individual affirmation into collective purpose. And in this web of reflection, love transforms into a bridge—a luminous thread connecting the innermost self to the vastness of the world.

Suffer silently in bitter solitude,
Where the sugars of soul ferment.
Reason can always get stronger,
But lighter are the best scents.

To approach this issue from another perspective, imagine a factory worker waking up at 7 a.m. every morning, driving to the factory, and spending their entire day packing food items until 6 p.m. Why would this person do that? Are they not a free individual, capable of choosing how to spend their life? If freedom exists, then why choose a life confined to repetitive labor? Is poverty not preferable to the monotony of packing food all day? Could living with a hunter-gatherer tribe in the Amazon rainforest, with all its unpredictability and vitality, not offer a more enriching existence than such regimented labor? This absurdity demands explanation. The factory worker endures this life because they are striving to make money to achieve a specific goal. That goal serves as an abstracted means to something else they desire, and that desire is yet another layer of abstraction tracing back to the thing they love. If you follow this convoluted thread of reasoning to its source, it becomes clear: they love themselves. This self-love reflects outward, guiding their actions toward supporting someone or something else they care for. However, the worker's ignorance—perhaps a lack of access to education or other opportunities—narrows their options, making factory labor the most straightforward way to obtain resources. In this light, it is love, intertwined with ignorance, that renders this apparent absurdity sensible.

Having achieved the capability to control my own emotions,
I end up, many a time, choosing to not feel any negative emotion.
Does this have drawbacks I am unaware of?
Could the bad be as valuable as the good feelings?
Without the bad, are we truly living?

But this raises an uncomfortable truth: there are more efficient, less labor-intensive, and scalable ways to generate wealth than performing menial labor in a factory. Most factory labor persists not out of necessity but because a high population of undereducated individuals keeps wages low. This economic reality makes it less urgent or appealing for industrialists to invest in robotics or automation. Paradoxically, if one conducted proper financial modeling, the long-term profitability of amortized robotics investments would become evident and obvious. Robots, after all, do not tire, require breaks, or endure the emotional burdens of separation from family. Yet, the short-sightedness and fear of industrialists maintain this system, perpetuating reliance on human labor. The truth is this: human menial labor is not essential for an advanced economy. Anyone arguing otherwise is clinging to a myopic view. Anything a human can do in a factory, a well-designed robot can perform more efficiently, inexpensively, and without the human toll. Robots will never miss a shift, never suffer, and never leave children waiting for them at home. And yet, the fear persists —"What will happen when robots take our jobs?" The answer lies in the inevitable optimization of the economy. With widespread automation, corporations will accumulate such vast reserves of excess capital that they will have no choice but to reinvest in areas requiring human creativity and sensitivity —art, marketing, and endeavors that demand the nuance of human judgment. Personally, I would rather be the individual supervising the robots than the one performing the tasks they replace. Perhaps that is just my perspective, but I believe it is one worth considering.

To the teachers. The pullers which pull us from indirection,
Which pull us to clean air, to life born strong and healthy.

To scholarship, eternity is what?
A searching, a craving for deep intellectual power.
Though, can you find true love when you search for power?
Material power is servile and pusillanimous to life's mechanics.

My love must learn to move on from eternity.
My love must not get too prideful, such that it cannot sink down to the limited and material.
Unworthy ears hear no richness in such contradictions.

In the relationships between people, the link of love bears a striking resemblance to the relationship between humans and art. Art is the material embodiment of human love, just as humans themselves are manifestations of love in a physical form. Healthy, authentic art emerges as the overflow from a person's internal reservoir of love. Similarly, in the most fulfilling relationships, love flows outward from the excess of self-love within each individual. A parent's love for their child mirrors the artist's love for their craft; the overflow of affection and care shapes the child, leaving imprints as a sculptor molds clay. However, just as some artists deplete themselves unsustainably, creating without replenishing their inner reserves, some parents or caregivers fail to nurture their own self-love. These individuals create cracks in their proverbial cups, leading to burnout, mental health crises, or an inability to sustainably care for those they love. Without first loving yourself fully, you cannot sustain the love you pour into others. The well must be replenished, the cup filled to the brim, before its excess can spill outward in healthy and lasting ways. Love, in all its manifestations—whether for art, labor, or people—thrives only when it is rooted in abundance, nurtured at its source, and shared as an unforced overflow.

If mediocrity does not bring you to your knees,
if it does not well up tears and break your refrain to weep,
if escaping it does not compete with the desire to breathe,
it will be impossible to unravel its claws masked by the cushioned seat.

TOWARDS A STRONGER LIFE AFFIRMATION, A DEEPER PHILAUTIA

Why does life exist? Love.
What do we live for? Love.
These answers—these tools,
this poetry—
are what raise the strongest people.

What has wisdom borne unto us, this deep and brooding wisdom that rises from the tenebrous pools where few dare wade? It whispers its secrets in the language of emperors, the language of farmers, shaping us into sovereigns not of dominion, but of essence. It teaches that gold is but the harlot's hymn, the merchant's prison, seductive yet hollow, for when the gleam of riches fades and the gilded idols crumble, it is the soil beneath our feet that answers to the sun's caress. To be a king —is it not to seek the finest fruits of life for oneself, to offer to one's brother only the second sweetest, and to the stranger, the excess? What the privileged are taught, though the heart recoils at its simplicity, its cruelty. For what sustains us? Not crowns nor coins, but the rhythm of days renewing themselves as the river carves its path through stone, neither asking nor offering permission. Only the soil, rain, and sun deserve our allegiance, our ingenuity, our toil. To rule in silence, to plant where others seek to profit and to reap with reverence for the unyielding cycles that cradle us.

Once I learned of my illness,
Every attempt to soothe it
Has been fruitless and frivolous.
Every person who I have been blessed to impression,
I have, to a degree, infected with its contagion.
My hands grasp and dig into the sand,
Sinking deeper, the more I struggle,
The less I can withstand.
A condition never to become stable,
Once contracted,
Love unfortunately is incurable.

What is self-love? Self-love means not blaming yourself while also avoiding self-pity, both in general and when those goals are not achieved. Self-love involves embracing your imperfections and learning from setbacks rather than wallowing in regret. It is affirming your desires and transforming them into actionable goals, with an understanding of the sacrifices required to achieve them. Self-love acknowledges that setbacks are part of the process and that they do not diminish your worth. It is feeling sadness and loss when faced with failure but learning to forgive yourself. Forgiving yourself involves reflecting on mistakes, learning from them, and then moving forward with compassion. Self-love involves building resilience while also knowing when to let go of the past—what might be called the art of forgetting. To forget, to know learning is not always a benefit, learning how to unlearn, is deep wisdom. Self-love is treating yourself with respect, dignity, and fairness. It means understanding that your past does not define your future, and that you have the power to shape who you are actively in your becoming.

Wished for nothing,
I blow out my candles.
Silence in my heart,
A burden of ingratitude
Few others have handled.
Knocked to my knees,
Forgiveness I shan't plead.
Whatever above I do not praise,
For the heeded do not pray.
Wholeness does not rattle.

Self-love also requires openness—allowing others into your life, even when this brings the risk of pain, as part of finding the right people for you. This openness is essential because it helps you create connections that can nurture you, but it must be balanced with discernment to protect your boundaries. Attempting to compare different kinds of true love is pointless, much like comparing types of drinking water. While there may be subtle differences in flavor, all love (apart from harmful distortions) shares a common essence. True love, whether romantic, familial, or self-love, carries the same core value: acceptance and care. This does not imply that all reality is made of the same substance, as such a reductionist view is unnecessary. Instead, we must recognize that self-love is essential for engaging in any form of relational love. Loving another person stems from the overflow of love within yourself; without a foundation of self-love, you cannot sustainably love another. Without this inner foundation, love can become reliant on external validation rather than a healthy, reciprocal exchange.

And there before me lies the button
To repeat it over and over again.
Every millisecond and every atom.
I need not touch such a button,
For it already has broken.
On it, the weight of my love has fallen.

When describing self-love, it needs to be meticulously separated from Narcissism. Narcissism is rooted in delighting in your material qualities, such as physical beauty, intelligence, athleticism, social status, or business success. These qualities, even intellectual ones, are tied to the material interactions of the body, and they focus on the external rather than the internal. True self-love, by contrast, means finding joy in yourself and your life, even when your outward qualities may seem lacking. This joy comes from an inner sense of worth and acceptance, not contingent on the fluctuating judgments of others or society's standards. The hallmark of a great business is its ability to function and grow without constant involvement from its founder. Similarly, the hallmark of great self-love is its capacity to operate and flourish without requiring continuous conscious attention. This allows you to focus your liberated energy on external goals and relationships. Self-love, once developed, no longer needs constant, active cultivation. Just as a healthy business can run efficiently with minimal intervention, self-love becomes a sustaining force that propels you forward, freeing you to invest in the world around you.
In the early stages, both businesses and self-love require significant attention to build a strong foundation. This foundation involves practices such as self-reflection, self-compassion, and mindfulness. If your self-love is not functioning properly, you must dedicate time and effort to nurture it. This nurturing can take the form of journaling,

therapy, meditation, or any practice that helps you align with your true self. Once you establish a working model of self-love, it can grow and operate in the background, allowing you to shift your attention outward. The key is to develop a sustainable practice that continues to nourish you even when you are focused on other aspects of life. When you cultivate self-love and heal internally, you transcend the limitations of self-centeredness. It is important to recognize that self-love is not about indulging in selfishness or disregarding the needs of others. Rather, it allows you to love and care for others from a place of fullness, without depletion.

A love so terribly hollow,
Careful knocks return wooded echoes,
Evidently too—shallow.
My lead stamps aground upon the prow.
Through the ripples of their muddled water,
They think their shimmering coins have value.

There is something about a fountain.

It brings me to disgust at the thought to swim,
While there are some dark, cavernous rivers,
Where a thousand calls gush to jump within.
Interesting how the deeper, dangerous unknown
Can have so many more attractive tones.

Unconditional self-love does not equate to toxic positivity. Instead, it is about embracing yourself without judgment, regardless of your circumstances. This love acknowledges past hardships and encourages you to confront and address them, all while maintaining unwavering self-acceptance. It is about accepting that challenges are a part of life, but they do not diminish your value.

A poet repeats himself—
Not from madness,
But when what is written
Must be read multiple times.
Although when you sing, sing a common night's song,
Your voice. Oh darling. Spilling of expression—
So few words— A poet has much of to be ashamed.

Love, when detached from material reality, refrains from judging your life's circumstances. It does not justify unacceptable past events or situations, but it encourages you to see them for what they are—part of your story, not your identity. Rather, it motivates you to engage with the material world and address your challenges while continuing to love yourself, irrespective of the outcomes. This means that even in difficult times, your love for yourself remains a constant, helping you navigate adversity without being consumed by it.
Is love egotistical? Is it an act of the ego or the id? System 1 or System 2? Love exists wherever there is something capable of affirmation. The ego may shape love and direct its outward expression, but the id—the primal, untamed essence of the self—is the engine room of its boundless capacity. However, more research is needed on this conception of the brain and the mind, as it risks becoming another forced classification or "spook." The maturation of a person is marked by the ripening of their love. How many men have I seen doomed to immaturity, their love stunted, unripe, forever caught in the clutches of fear or selfishness? From the many philosophies that have attempted to define life—egoism, nihilism, moralism, and the like—I find myself drawn to a singular truth. What does that make me, then? Not an egoist, not a nihilist, but a lovist! One who believes in love as the highest principle.

There in my heart,
an amulet and its song,
opens, twirling as it starts,
and again, the wind blows,
and again, the sun shines.
Another river of pain flows—
dare to cross mine?

Consider the myth of Prometheus. At first glance, it is a tale of punishment, of the undesirable consequences of defying the gods. But delving deeper: if an entity were truly immortal, it would not feel pain, for pain is an evolutionary mechanism, an alarm signaling the risk of death. A god, immune to mortality, has no use for such alarms. Prometheus, therefore, should not feel the agony of the eagle devouring his liver. Yet the myth insists on his suffering, a suffering that must be examined not as divine retribution but as a reflection of the human condition. A titan or god, incapable of death, is also incapable of love. Without mortality, there is no urgency, no preciousness to existence. The god persists, but it does not choose to; it cannot embrace or affirm life because there is no alternative. Its existence is a prison, unmarked by the freedom and vitality that are the luxuries of mortal beings.

For the gods in Greek myths are representations of the attributes in humans that remain eternal across generations. For this reason, it is necessary to provide stories about the failures and successes of these anthropomorphic gods so that their mistakes are not repeated. Thus, the gods feel pain, for the experience of pain is consistent with human life across time. Prometheus, in enduring the eagle's torment, becomes not just a hero but a poet of existence. Pain, the raw and visceral teacher, drags us from ignorance to profundity. It is through suffering that he transcends his defiance and achieves a profound affirmation of life. Not for the fire he gave to humanity but for his ability to endure, to learn, and to affirm even in torment, Prometheus stands as a symbol of love's unyielding resilience when he is anthropomorphized as a titan who feels pain.

And what of Icarus, whose myth warns us against hubris, against the folly of flying too close to the sun? The common interpretation urges moderation, temperance, the careful avoidance of extremes. But let us pause. Where does temperance end, if not upon the shores of fear? Fear of offense, fear of failure, fear of death. The true philosophical principle, towering above this moderation, is the rejection of fear itself. To fear death is to chain oneself to mediocrity. Alexander of Macedon—did he not live without moderation, without temperance, and in doing so, carve his name into the stone of eternity?

Of grasping toward gods,
    As one gets closer, his skin burns,
    His bones melt, logic bends and recurses
To reject earthly forms.

Ascending upwards, the sun warms his skin,
Unknowingly melting the wax of his wings.
    In search of light, he fell to his death—
A moth in an ocean of flames and sparks.

Few will understand that it takes more courage
To stay in the dark.

Icarus did not die because he was foolish; he died because he was free. His ascent, reckless and magnificent, was a declaration of defiance against the finite. In the eternal recurrence of all things, to reach for the sun is to affirm life in its most radiant, fleeting beauty. To rise, to burn, to fall—this is the essence of existence. Higher is the man who reaches up to the sun; however, exalted is the man who looks down. Stares carefully from the heights of love into the detailed beauty of life. The philosopher Icarus becomes a symbol not of failure but of transcendence. As man ascends toward the eternal, his finite consciousness begins to unravel, the material trappings of his being dissolve. This is not destruction but dematerialization— a return to essence, a confrontation with the infinite. Death, then, is not the end but the necessary dissolution that allows us to grasp the eternal. Inherent in the recklessness of Icarus is an affirmation of life and its beauty. His recklessness is the understanding that death is something deserving of contempt —that is the core of philosophy. If Icarus successfully crossed the ocean, eternal recurrence and the oscillation of the universe demand that all permutations of Icarus' story must exist, including an infinite number of other lives in which he died, and vice versa. Prometheus represents endurance, while Icarus represents transience. Could both be perfect representations of self-love?

To love, to suffer, to strive, to rise and fall—this is the poetry of existence. It is not the denial of death but the embrace of it allows us to truly live. Prometheus and Icarus, in their myths, remind us that love, and freedom are bound by the same thread: the refusal to be imprisoned by fear. In their struggles and in their defiance, they teach us what it means to affirm life, to burn brightly, and to leave behind the dim comfort of the ordinary.

You think I could bleed this poetry
Without birth into wretched poverty
Like love it is simultaneously
A state of illness and blessedness.

Torment and dread, tempest of childhood,
poverty can exist spiritually,
materially, and experientially.
Over many an edge, I have stood.

The Christian sentiment of loving your neighbor misses the mark when it comes to the true, profound nature of genuine love. It asserts that loving others is more important than oneself, but it ignores the foundational truth one can never love another if they have not yet learned how to tenderly love themselves. If you cannot cook for yourself a good meal why should you cook for another? If you only know how to hurt yourself how can you be expected to properly care for another? To love another more than you love yourself is, quite simply, a lie, a fatal imbalance. For one, it is impossible to prove that the other person even exists in their entirety, for you only know them through the veil of your own perception. How, then, can you claim to love what you cannot fully know? If your own cup is empty, how can you pour to fill another's? If you do not love yourself adequately, you will not have the strength, the capacity, nor the clarity to truly love another. The love that you give must always overflow from a cup brimming with self-love. You cannot spill more from the cup than what is inside it. If your cup is not full, if you do not love yourself fully, you cannot fully love anyone else. Love is a reflection of the depth of your own soul, a mirror that cannot reflect anything deeper than the image it holds. Another person exists for you only through the lens of your perception, and while you may rigorously perceive that the other person exists, your perception is finite, inherently limited, and will never capture the infinity of the person before you. The person you engage with is always an interpretation, a shadow of their full self, an imperfect, reductive version of their infinite divinity. To reduce the fullness of their being to mere traits, behaviors, or qualities is an injustice—an incomplete representation of their true essence. Only a god knows existence in its entirety, for a god does not perceive, but KNOWS in truth. To desire to know the truth of existence is to aspire to divinity, but such an aspiration is both futile and vainglorious. We can never achieve such knowledge, not while we remain in our fragile, finite forms. If you love others more than you love yourself, the river of your soul will eventually drain your reservoirs, running your lakes dry. A dry lake is not just an absence of water—it is the precursor to death, a death that could have been prevented, had you cared for your own heart first.

You think can you,
Cut and hurt me anew?
Possible, but you let me heal true,
And scar tissue is tougher to cut through.

To love another, then, is to be full enough to love without expectation, without need, to pour from the overflow of self-love. Without this, love becomes a transaction, an attempt to consume the other to fill an inner void. If I am jealous of another person's possessions, I may attempt to take them, to steal or destroy the thing that I covet. But if I am envious of the love they possess, how do I steal that? How do I claim their capacity for love as my own? I cannot kill them, for that would only strip me of the very opportunity to learn from them. To truly understand the love they embody, I must do the opposite of destroying them. I must support them, engage with them kindly, seek to understand the source of their love by interacting with them in ways that nurture both of our spirits. Since the rise of industrialization and the pervasive grip of modernization, there has been a dilution of the divine essence in human love. Producing more people, and improving material life such that there is mor access to indulgence and decadence has become a dilutive process.

A cut by which I have no intention to stitch,
Time slips from my fingers, like water and the finest sand.
I grasp and grasp, yet the more I squeeze, the more escapes my hand.
As the breeze falters upon the glade,
just as you have to my soul, my dear,
and the love in my heart fades,
a love now insecure, I fear.

When we view love as eternal, as something not bound to the fleeting material world, the comparison of one person's life to another's becomes utterly irrelevant. A person may possess every material advantage—wealth, beauty, success—but without true love, these things are empty, hollow vessels. They cannot fulfill the deepest needs of the soul, nor can they realize the richness of a human heart. In fact, someone who has everything materially but lacks internal love will experience life as nothing but a dry shell, a body stumbling through time without purpose. Envying another person for their material privilege, even when they seem to possess every material perfection, is akin to wishing for a death of the soul. Such envy stems from a profound misunderstanding of what truly nourishes us. Depression, that most terrible of afflictions, is always linked to inadequate love, to the absence of true self-affirmation. It is in these moments, when the soul is depleted and the heart weary, that the person realizes they are starving for the very love they failed to cultivate within themselves. The only thing worth envying in another person is the depth of love they have attained, the embodiment of love they so fully realize. My envy, then, is not a desire to take what they have, but a call to action within myself. It is a prompt to love more, to love deeper, to love better. Their love is not something I can steal, imitate, or trade—it must be earned, won, and produced through my own effort.

What have the poets taught me?
To open myself up and to not excuse my fear, my slavery.

I was always inclined to write lines to rationalize courage

A line like:
If you kill me, I will just come back again,
Come back again in different form, but spirit the same,

Lines like:
Since what is inside will always stay alive.
I will never truly die, even if my physical body does.

But what if courage does not need to be rationalized,
What if courage was always just madness herself.
She can only be described and explained in surface,
But every embodiment will be perfect and absolute,

If when I die there will be nothing uniquely the same again.
The world will lose nothing since it never had me to obtain.
In pursuit of being my own, and always never fully grown.
If one day I am gone fully and if I die, fully
Without all the spiritual rigamarole or other nonsense,
My spirit is gone too. Everything ends as back to before it started.
There is nothing worth weeping over, as I lived true to myself, undistorted.

In this framework of eternal love, life's material quality becomes irrelevant. It becomes a mere backdrop to the magnificence of love. Whether I live five years, tragically cut short by leukemia, or whether I live a long and prosperous life, reaching ninety-five with children and grandchildren by my side, my love remains equally full, equally divine. Every moment of those five years is just as sacred, just as hallowed as the decades of a man whose life is with material wealth and fulfilled desires. Love is not measured in the span of days, nor in the fulfillment of material desires, but in the affirmation of existence, in the eternal embrace of love that transcends time. What is the difference between these two lives? One is shorter, and the other longer. One is marked by greater material success, and the other by lesser. But the one constant, the eternal truth that binds both lives, is the perfect affirmation of consciousness. In the eyes of love, no moment is greater than another; every moment is just as full, just as perfect, just as noble.

The great philosophers, those who have achieved such heights through their spiritual endeavors, know this truth well. They have not only clambered up the pyramid of divinity—they have learned to kneel before it, to bend their hearts in humble submission to the mysteries of the universe. And they know that to confront love is to confront a dangerous, beautiful god. To upset this god is not to fear the torment that may follow, but to risk the loss of presence, of being in the very moment of suffering. For when that failure comes—and it will come, as surely as night follows day—it is not the torment that is most unbearable, but the solitude. When the darkness descends, when the stars fail to guide, when the food is tasteless and the sky bears down on your shoulders, the only love that will remain is the love you give to yourself. And in that moment, it is not the world that can save you, but the quiet, unfathomable depth of your own heart, the unshakable love you have cultivated for yourself. It is then that you understand: love, when true, is eternal.

Ten thousand suns,
Ten thousand suns,
you can barely see some shining
when my love comes a' fighting.

LIFE PERFORMANCE WITH A NOVEL CONCEPTION OF LOVE

Intelligence is not merely a capability of the human mind; it is a fundamental process inherent to life itself. In artificial intelligence, there is typically a model paired with an optimization method to improve that model. Similarly, as physical organic life forms, our bodies are phenotype models defined by genetic information. These models are then optimized through environmental feedback, natural selection, and internal development. This ongoing adaptation ensures that life remains resilient and capable of persisting under dynamic environmental conditions and shifting preferences of sexual partners. Life's optimization process can be likened to sprinting as fast as possible while staying in place—a relentless struggle for balance, survival, and reproduction. Even when no long-term improvement is achieved, the act of optimizing itself reflects an intelligent process at work. In this sense, intelligence is not confined to success or progress but exists wherever life actively responds to its challenges. If artificial intelligence is a product of the human mind—a creation born of the natural world—then it is simply another form of intelligence produced by nature. It is as natural as an apple tree or corn, both of which, paradoxically, are the result of humanity shaping nature to serve specific purposes.

My love, the stars they glisten so far.
I am afraid we are alone in this darkness splitting apparition
God made this stage in this theatre
So, we can dance for another's pleasure.
Is it not better that we dance together?
Even though I have you to hold and to listen,
why is it still so deeply I suffer?
For it is through the gravest moments of despair
I have only the void as company,
I have only the void into which to stare
You have no truth. An only through my interpretation.
Your connection is but a hallucination,
Indebted to endure, and pretend to accept, deep isolation.

My Love, the stars they glisten so far,
Yet, what would they be without our perception?!
The universe has created our inner light because it yearns to feel itself through us.
Existing as the burning white constellations for it was not enough.

This view blurs the distinction between what we traditionally label as artificial and natural, challenging deeply ingrained dichotomies. Furthermore, the intelligence of the natural world operates independently of human definitions or understanding of intelligence. However, our ability to comprehend these forms of intelligence is inherently limited by the anthropocentric nature of our language and perspective. As a result, whether we study biological intelligence or artificial intelligence, our understanding will always be filtered through the subjective lens of human experience.

Ten thousand ounces of gratitude
For every crude adversity —
pounces opportunity to prove
A love of unbounded quantity,
And their hasty laughs misconstrued,
without life's given purpose,
The wells of love show torrid surface,
Though once tapped —
make most divine adversaries nervous.

Intelligence, understood as the optimization of a model to perform under perceived conditions, is not always beneficial to the entity exhibiting it. New information and conditions can emerge in an environment, potentially rendering previously learned adaptations obsolete. For example, a predator optimized to hunt a specific prey may struggle if that prey becomes scarce or evolves new defenses. If a model becomes overly sensitive or rigid in response to prior learning, it may struggle to adapt to novel conditions that contradict its earlier adaptations. This limitation highlights the importance of balancing flexibility versus obstinance in intelligence. Thus, knowing when not to learn—or when to forget—is just as vital as learning. This prevents biological models from overfitting to their environments. For this reason, we learn slowly, act cautiously, and question before accepting.

Nobody may love you now,
Although, in the end,
all that matters, is if you love yourself.

You may have achieved every goal,
With not a single desire left,
You may have moved on from everyone else,

But only an inward forgiveness
Will heal the deepening coastal shelf.

The preservation and perseverance of life depend on actions aligned with the current material conditions we and other life forms inhabit. It can be evolutionarily advantageous to act without love. The person who exist well integrated into the material realm is exposed to the most information and has the best intuition about the material world. This can be a huge advantage to winning in the material world. The problem for these kinds of people is that they are deeply unprepared for handling adversity, as there is no spiritual realm for them to tap into when facing absurdity. In a purely natural context, actions are driven by survival and reproduction rather than by moral considerations. In nature, there are no inherently evil actions; such actions often go unpunished and may benefit the organisms that commit them. A parasite, for example, consumes its host without moral consequence; there is no universal retribution condemning parasites to hell. This absence of moral judgment in nature reflects the impartiality of natural processes, which prioritize outcomes over intentions.

The farmer and the soldier
Have more than
The trader and the philosopher.
For the former's focus
Is firmly nestled in life.
The latter cares only for fruitless theory.
The latter cares only for conveniences.
They bore life more than they please it.
In the philosopher's world of forms,
Life is always reduced to semblances.

By creating a state, humans can construct artificial

environments that punish "evil" actions, fostering trust within society. This trust allows individuals to feel secure enough to start businesses and make long-term investments, ultimately improving the ease and quality of life. Unlike the impartiality of nature, human societies impose moral frameworks to regulate behavior and promote collective well-being. However, from a philosophical perspective, improving material conditions may not enhance the intangible experience of life. While societal advancements provide comfort and security, they may not fulfill the deeper yearning for simplicity, freedom, and connection to nature that antiquity provides us. If you wish to live a materially successful life, take actions subservient to life itself: work hard, remain cold and rational, and make decisions that optimize success. This approach aligns with the practical necessities of survival and prosperity. I hope you fill your tomb full of valuables! If, however, you seek a fulfilling experiential life, you must learn to love—a mastery that transcends material existence. Love represents an embrace of the intangible, an acknowledgment of experiences that go beyond mere survival. To clarify, I do not advocate for either life or love as superior paths. Each person may choose their preference for navigating existence. The aim here is to present a novel perspective, not to assert that one way of life is better than another.

What happened to her?
She's gone.
What did you do to her?
I sacrificed her.

We humans, as life forms, are intricately designed to serve the processes of life itself. This design is not arbitrary; it reflects the fundamental reality that survival demands adherence to material conditions and biological imperatives. If we were to act solely out of love, disregarding material reality entirely, we would degrade and perish swiftly. However, humans occupy a unique position in the natural world. Unlike other organisms that act primarily based on instinct and genetic programming, we possess the capacity for abstract thought. This capability allows us to transcend purely biological programming and perform actions that arise from ideology, values, and love.

The sun.
It beats me down,
And warms me.

Love, understood as the unconditional affirmation of life, is an abstract construct—a product of the human mind capable of ideation beyond mere survival. In certain circumstances, humans can integrate love into their material pursuits, creating a harmony between the spiritual and biological aspects of existence. This integration can enhance both our internal, experiential lives and our external, material realities. Yet, life is an exceedingly complex system, where the causal relationships between actions and outcomes often remain elusive. Unlike the controlled settings of empirical experiments, real-world dynamics are unpredictable. Thus, acting unconditionally from love can produce outcomes just as favorable—or unfavorable—as acting with Darwinian optimization. This introduces the paradox that unconditional love, which seemingly defies logical material advantage, can still result in outcomes that align with survival and fulfillment. What matters most is that you act in accordance with your own sense of good taste, as this reflects a form of self-love—the only love that is verifiable. The seeming contradiction in suggesting love's transcendence and its relevance to material life is resolved when we consider that love's abstract nature influences the intentions behind actions, even as those actions operate within the material domain. Love is distinct from learning. It does not adapt or respond to the fluctuations of reality.

Rome fell from a false conception of Jove.
He does not care for war or riches,
Instead in his profound shallowness, simply
Takes what's he wants, kills what he hates
The ignorant and philistine sees it evil.
For they think evil cannot be born out of love.

It remains steadfast, unchanging, indivisible, and immune to the perturbations of material conditions. For this reason, human existence requires a delicate balance between learning from the material world and adhering to the unyielding nature of love. Through this balance, we navigate the duality of our existence as beings bound by biology yet capable of reaching for the transcendent. The expression of love is possible only through theoretical thought and consciousness. While animals may exhibit behaviors that appear loving—such as a mother bird risking her life to protect her hatchlings—these actions are fundamentally preprogrammed by genetic information because they confer evolutionary advantages. Love, however, is not about care, passion, or even value. It is the removal of conditions and valuations from thought, a transcendence of the material into the divine. It is not contingent upon outcomes or reciprocation. It is pure affirmation, free from the calculations of benefit or loss. Everything we hold dear as human beings is, in some way, a testament to love. The act of continuing life, the choices to mitigate risks, and the decision to raise children are expressions of this affirmation. While our genetic programming includes mechanisms like the death drive, which compels organisms toward entropy, the refusal of this drive is an act of defiance and love. To embrace the uncertainty and ambiguity of life, to undertake the daunting responsibility of child-rearing, and to persist in the face of inevitable mortality are all acts of profound love. These choices, though seemingly ordinary, represent a conscious rejection of despair and an affirmation of existence. They illustrate how love, even when it operates in mundane contexts, is a force that transcends mere survival and connects us to something greater.

Many only see forms,
They see value, utility,
They see their finished tables and soft beds,
The big buildings and little sheds.
They build and slave for that comfort feelin',
And when heat touches their skin,
They shift and squirm.

Few come along,
Seeing nothing of the sort,
Instead, seeing what to others
Is only heard in song.
They see the gods and spirits
Everywhere—how well they comport—
Enjoying themselves, dancing in the air.

When they see an eternal poet,
Their eyes open wide,
having never seen another glow inside.

This brings us to the relationship between love and faith. While deeply connected, they are not the same. Faith, in this context, is not necessarily belief in God but rather a belief in oneself and the world—a refusal to surrender, a conviction to keep going. Faith often arises from a form of defiance, a contempt for the material world, and, by extension, for death itself. This defiance stems from the recognition that death, as the ultimate cessation of material existence, is antithetical to life's perpetuation. However, faith can also stem from trust and hope, representing an alignment with life's broader continuity. These dual origins of faith—defiance and trust—highlight its complex relationship with the human condition.

The gods rarely descend
Upon the canaille.
When they do,
The blood pools,
The heads pile.
In divine solitude,
The gods casually
Lounge and shine.

Yet, while faith is powerful, it is not equal in strength or wisdom to love. Faith is akin to hope; it carries an expectation that the future will be as good as, if not better than, the present. Love, by contrast, makes no such speculations. It exists independently of outcomes or expectations. Love does not hinge on the promise of improvement or stability. It affirms every moment, even those destined to be filled with suffering or destitution. Pure love pays no heed to the ebb and flow of material reality. It is absolute, unshaken by despair or loss. To love in this way is to embrace life without conditions. When faced with the prospect of quitting, I would rather reject it out of love than out of faith. Faith, rooted in expectation, falters when those expectations are unmet. Love, however, endures unconditionally, its strength untouched by the tides of fortune or misfortune. To love is to reject resignation not because you anticipate triumph but because you affirm life itself, irrespective of what lies ahead. This rejection of resignation, grounded in love, embodies humanity's highest potential—to affirm existence without needing justification or assurance.

Someone may be watching,
Someone may be watching,
Whether my personal god,
Or some smoking bystander coughing,

Or myself in the mirror,
Always silent apart from the occasional laughter
Even if just the passing glance
Onto the burning ashes raindrops still fall after
Another opportunity, another chance.

Should I be ashamed of my hatred?
My owned experience of pining and yearning?
Tell me of a desire not sacred.
Tell me of a desire not worth beautifying.

Soon will be the furious cracking of lighting,
When poetry turns the moon blood red,
And the quetzal feathers shed,
off the basilisk's head.

It is evident from countless investigations that love does not concern itself with what is expedient for life. Yet, existence in this crude reality of ours is only made possible through love. To continue existing, one must love. This truth is something that most readers instinctively know in their hearts, even if it only needs to be articulated for clarity. If one's goal in reading and in life is to find an aesthetically pleasing partner, accumulate wealth, and gain power, such pursuits must be made coldly and without love. However, once these goals are achieved in the name of "the pursuit of happiness," a person will be left unfulfilled, and their heart will feel empty. They may come to believe that their life is meaningless. And while it's true that life might seem meaningless at times, this assertion is irrelevant to a life lived with an abundance of love. Love transcends such trivial concerns.

What have you seen of famine and disease?
Have you seen the skull piles?
Have you seen the blood seas?

By exploring novel definitions of love, we can cultivate deeper understandings of life and develop more profound frameworks for making decisions. If someone defines love simply as caring for another, they may reduce it to material support—providing a safe home, access to utilities, and comforts. For example, sending a grandmother to a nursing home while neglecting her otherwise, though pragmatic in preserving her life, may not fully express love. It is better described as a form of social reciprocity, as your grandmother is the one responsible in part for your life. True love is choosing to care for someone despite all the reasons not to. It's standing by their side even when there is no personal benefit, offering your support without expectation of reward. It's remaining present even when it costs you—whether in money, social status, or the many inconveniences life may throw your way—embracing these as sacrifices for their well-being. That is the essence of love. Of course, this must be balanced with self-love, as there comes a point were sacrificing for another impedes your ability to love yourself.

Ilium won Helen
Rome won the Mediterranean
Which is more beautiful?
If you had to choose
Which, would you? Personally,
I'm not so picky with woman.

Love is reflected in the quality of one's actions and presence, not merely in fulfilling functional roles. Love offers a richer, more vibrant way to understand life—one that can make a person anti-fragile, allowing them to grow from the challenges they face rather than be defeated by them. From these reflections, it becomes clear that a higher performance of life is a deeply complex endeavor, a balance between serving life's practical purposes—such as self-preservation or material growth—and engaging in what might be called eternal love or unconditional affirmation. This balance involves both rationality and irrationality. Love, by its very nature, is an irrational process. It does not always follow the rules of logic, yet it is foundational to our being.

Human relationships are central to the human experience, and a wise person must recognize that those they interact with are also biological beings, driven by their own corporeal instincts and serving life's biological imperatives. A person capable of true love is one who also possesses the rare ability for abstract thought, a gift that is surprisingly rare to find. To navigate life effectively and safely, it is practical to assume that others will act in their biological self-interest. This assumption shields us from disappointment, allowing us to be pleasantly surprised when someone expresses pure, untainted love. A truly wise person crafts their life in such a way that, if their love were to disappear, the world would still be too beautiful and meaningful to abandon. This wisdom stems from an understanding that love does not depend on external circumstances. Once one learns to fill their heart with love, regardless of what happens in the material world, their consciousness becomes unshaken. Their sense of self—of individuality, of presence—is not dependent on the fluctuations of life's fortunes but on the unchanging reservoir of love within them. In this way, a person is free from the material reality that others are so attached to. The more love one carries, the less their emotional and mental states are swayed by the good or bad events that occur in their lives.

Who then is the ideal lover? The ideal lover does not allow their wax wings to burn under the sun of eternal love. Instead, they maintain a balance between unconditional love and the conditional realities of life. The ideal lover serves life by staying in perfect health, understanding that their well-being is not only a personal responsibility but a means to continue expressing love. This balance is essential because love, when expressed through a fragile body, can only be sustained as long as that body remains capable of carrying out loving actions. If they do not have perfect health, they will work diligently to achieve it. And if they are suffering from an unfixable illness, they will use every moment to either find joy in life while it lasts or seek out novel paths to a cure. The ideal lover can endure every malice, every disrespect, and every adversity, paying them no heed—because what do material consequences matter to a perfect conscious love?

Down the mountains
I bring the gift of danger
    to the lowlander
Sacrifices at the river.
    When the blood
    touches water it
Starts the cycling fountain
    of passion, and civilization.
My impatient love
    it overflows
In tidepools and streams.
    Incomprehensible
    when in prose.

Such love transcends the pain and limitations imposed by the physical world, seeing them as temporary conditions rather than defining aspects of existence. If the ideal lover is tortured, does that mean they will love themselves any less? No. Their love remains unshaken and perfect, unaffected by the physical or emotional torment they may endure. Love, when it is truly unconditional, does not waver in response to suffering; instead, it strengthens the resolve to continue living and loving. If they have every possession stripped from them, does that diminish their will to continue living through eternal love? Again, no. The loss of material things is of little consequence to the ideal lover, for they understand that love is not bound by possessions or external circumstances. If aliens were to abduct them and force them to live forever, torturing them endlessly, they would endure it forever, for love is their guiding force. And when the aliens ask, "Why don't you prefer death?" the ideal lover would simply respond, "Because of love." This illustrates that love is not tied to life's comforts or its ease; rather, it exists as an eternal and unwavering force, enduring through all circumstances, even those of unimaginable hardship.

Every book I've read
is another me at another time,
reminding myself of something important.
Lives short and long, a thousand more deaths,
Every life a choice — you can choose to go next.
Rarely do I remember, but so be it in this one I do,
Calmly passing, each wave anew.

The ideal lover seeks to sustain themselves, to be prepared and protected against future challenges, not out of fear or greed, but simply so they can continue to live longer and express more love. They understand that more time alive means more opportunities to produce love, and they are not tempted to burn out through martyrdom. Let the martyrs be remembered in history books; the loving soul leaves an impact not through written words, but through the lasting impressions they leave upon material reality. Their influence is not recorded through hearsay, but through genuine action. The loving soul impresses their will upon the world, and death is not considered prudent for achieving those goals. This suggests that the ideal lover is not one who sacrifices their life in dramatic, fleeting gestures, but one who seeks to make a quiet, lasting difference, letting their love manifest through their actions and enduring presence.

Searching for truth?
I search for beauty.
We are brothers then!
Unequal brothers,
But brothers nonetheless.
I will caress your face at the pyre.
At the pyre, your face I will caress.
Fratricide makes the strongest empires.

In the grand tapestry of existence, the act of creation stands as the pinnacle of human endeavor, a testament to our deepest passions and aspirations. To create another person, another organism, is the highest art form one can perform. To bring forth life, to shape the raw clay of the universe into something uniquely our own, is an expression of love and purpose. It is through creation that we see the deepest expression of our will and our love; life is the ultimate masterpiece. The second highest form of art is to take life away, to kill. This may seem paradoxical, as taking life is usually seen as an act of destruction. However, it too holds a place in the complex web of existence, as it is a part of the balance of creation and destruction. Both of these actions carry serious moral implications, but love cannot be understood merely through moral evaluations. Love transcends morality; it is not bound by the right or wrong of actions, but by the intentions behind them and the deeper truth they reveal. This does not mean that love justifies every action, but rather that the essence of love seeks to understand the broader context and deeper meaning of what we do, even in acts that seem contradictory, like taking life.

Telling me love is pleasure

is telling me you never knew her.
A poem knows pain only in ignorance;
it knows not of love's true song and dance.

As taking life ranks second in beauty to creating it, so too does the prohibition against killing direct human energy toward other pursuits. When a person is artificially constrained from taking life, they are compelled to direct their energies toward the creation of other forms of art—literature, philosophy, painting, science, and so on. The profundity of the command "thou shall not kill" is not to suppress the human desire to destroy, but to refocus it on the creative, productizing the human spirit and its activities. This inevitably leads to the post-industrial world we live in, where everything is artificial, everything is designed and created by human hands. We have castrated the natural impulse to kill, and in doing so, we have removed the natural checks and balances that once governed our world. The unchecked progress of human creation has led to a world of excess, where everything is designed, yet nothing feels quite as natural or fulfilling. As the products of man grow uncontrollably, with no natural constraints, one must ask: is our world truly better now because of it? Is our excess productivity not the direct cause of our greatest existential threats today? As usual, we have helped a few at the cost of the many.

Every book I have read
Is another me at another time,
Reminding myself of something important.
Lives short and long, a thousand more deaths,
Every life a choice—you can choose to go next.
Rarely do I remember; so be it, in this one, I do—
Calmly passing, each wave anew.

In this dance of creation and destruction, we find the essence of our existence—a continuous cycle where each act of building is tempered by the necessity of letting go, of breaking down the old to make room for new life and love. This duality is not a contradiction, but a harmonious interplay, a symphony where each note of creation is balanced by a counterpoint of destruction. Each act of building is tempered by the necessity of deconstruction. In embracing this balance, we discover the true art of living: a life rich with meaning and depth, where every creation is cherished and every destruction understood as a step toward new beginnings. By accepting the cyclical nature of life, we come to understand that neither creation nor destruction is complete on its own. Each needs the other, and it is in the interweaving of both that we find the fullness of existence—love, purpose, and a deeper connection to the universe.

It does not shrivel from age;
it does not atrophy from disuse.
Neglect my love, and it is unaffected.
It only gets stronger
as my life goes on longer.

An entrepreneur who loves what they do affirms unconditionally their business or industry. This unconditional affirmation is an expression of higher love, even though it contains components that are utilitarian or money-seeking. Because the business owner loves what they do, they are more likely to weather the storms of hardship and persevere through adversity. In life, the longer you stay alive and remain an active player, the more opportunities you have to succeed. Life, in a game-theory sense, can be viewed as an infinitely repeating game. While this view may not fully capture the essence of life, it offers an interesting framework for exploring material success through love. In this context, dying is the worst possible outcome for a player in the game—not because dying is intrinsically bad, but because death means the player can no longer participate in the rounds of the game, reducing their probability of success to zero. So, how can one play as many rounds as possible to increase the chance of winning? By loving oneself, refusing to give up on pursuing material goals, and, most crucially, never ending one's life prematurely. The last point is the most significant. By loving yourself, you gain a greater ability to pick yourself up, dust yourself off, and try again. This is crucial in the pursuit of material success, as the path to achievement is rarely straightforward and often requires resilience. Life, however, is not merely a game. In truth, life is an art—a complex journey without objective truths. There are countless ways to live, different types of success, and often, the underdogs and those who defy conventions can outcompete others, because life, by its very nature, is unpredictable. This understanding invites a shift from a rigid, game-like strategy to a more dynamic, adaptable approach to living and succeeding.

Shush...
Listen to that.
Do you hear it?
It is love's experience.
Unveiling itself in silence.

Since love is both our primary cause and ultimate end, spirituality and morality can often be seen as misrepresentations of true love. In a world where the causes and effects of events are often unknown, and where the valuations of everything are uncertain, a person who acts out of true love will ultimately stand higher than one who is guided by faulty moral or spiritual valuations. Love, when pursued in its highest form, transcends conventional moral standards and spiritual dogmas. It operates not within the constraints of right and wrong, but in alignment with a deeper, more profound understanding of existence—one that sees beyond surface judgments and into the true essence of being. This deeper love is what shapes both individual actions and the broader course of life, moving beyond simple ethical constraints to a more holistic and transformative approach.

I too wept when I hath learned,
There was once Ilium, and it burned.

A 'good' person, as defined by many today, is often seen as virtuous and selfless—someone whose actions benefit the community or state more than themselves, altering the scale and impact of their deeds. The accumulation of such virtuous and selfless actions can lead to erratic results at the community level, but at the national level, it often contributes to the increasing power of the state. For instance, if someone devotes time to educate underprivileged children in their free time, this can improve the quality of life and productivity of those children, thereby contributing to the strength of the economy and the power of the state. These children may grow up to become professionals, business owners, and industrialists, contributing tax dollars to the state's operations. However, while the virtuous and selfless person may help people on the ground level, they are not in control of the actions of the state. The state is often held to limited accountability because few entities have the resources or power to challenge it. This results in the inevitable abuse of power, both domestically and internationally, and the concentration of authority in the hands of a few individuals, even in democratic systems. The state will use violence to protect its own authority and maintain control, regardless of the cost. Therefore, the 'good, selfless, virtuous' person must critically question the outcomes of their actions. Could the short-term "good" that they do ultimately result in long-term harm to humanity? The development of toxic gas, nuclear bombs, and industrial killing machines were all conceived by scientists and engineers who believed they were doing "good" for their countries. This raises an important question: perhaps humanity requires a more complex expression of love than simply performing "good actions." In fact, this prompts us to reconsider the idea of goodness itself, questioning whether simplistic moral frameworks are sufficient for navigating the complexity of our world and the potential consequences of our actions.

Every scribbled line,
I am not their cause either.
They are made by the reader.
The writer is fated to decline,
but the reader lives forever,
born recurrently through time.

Beauty provides another powerful example of greatness achieved by obediently serving the goals of life. Through the harsh conditions of sexual and environmental selection, humans have become naturally beautiful because beauty impacts competitiveness. However, beauty can also result from sheer luck. There is a common sentiment that one should be more attracted to a person's personality than their physical appearance. This sexual strategy may indeed improve mental health, both for individuals and their offspring. However, the issue is not as simple as it seems. If someone is beautiful not by chance but as a result of generations of careful selection, we see that beauty is not simply an arbitrary trait. Over many generations, the pursuit of beauty reflects forward-thinking decisions and sacrifices. To have beautiful children, one must find a beautiful partner, which requires patience and sacrifice. Searching for the right partner, often without guarantees of success, is no trivial matter. In this sense, a person's physical beauty can reflect hundreds of years of careful attention, decisions, and sacrifices—decisions made by ancestors whose influence remains significant even though they are not physically present in the moment. Just because you do not see your ancestors walking around today does not mean their actions are not still impacting the present. In many ways, ancestors are like gods—they are invisible, yet their influence is infinite, shaping our current reality in profound ways. They exist in our lives as both real and unreal, having an impact that transcends time. This deep, unseen influence provides the backdrop for the lives we lead today. We, as ancestors to future generations, similarly have an infinite influence on the future, making us gods in our own right. The actions we take today, guided by love and intentionality, will reverberate through time, shaping the lives of those who come after us. Our legacy, in this sense, is not only about material achievements but also about the love we pass down to future generations. Thus, in honoring our own legacies, we are also participating in an ongoing, timeless expression of love that will continue to impact the world long after we are gone.

For much time, I tried to create music.
Until I learned I was meant for poetry.
Music best created and listened to while buzzed.
Poesy is best read and forged in solemn sobriety.
Etched into eternity with blood.

The deeply loving person, who can completely disregard reality, allows their love to consume them from the inside out. They allow it to burn through their being, creating a fire that sears flesh and produces metallic smoke. Men need formal education in how to love, as their intuitions on love are often diverse and unreliably positive. While some may learn on their own how to channel their internal flames, if young men are not taught how to cultivate love, their unchecked anger may destroy everything they care about, searching for what a loveless life has never given them. *The young boy will burn his village to finally feel its warmth.* Women, on the other hand, appear to have a different relationship with love, but attending to their education is just as essential. We do not need any more Adonises and Aurelianos. The stronger women I have known in my life, have some intrinsic understanding of love. They seem to bathe in it daily, a quantity that would likely overwhelm most men. Their love forms the very bubbles in their baths, and they know how to control it. They can allow it to burn softly under the wind, ensuring it never risks being extinguished. This steady, controlled flame is sufficient to sustain them and will likely work as a valuable learning for many young men. Yet for some, this gentle warmth is often not enough to satisfy the relentless yearning that drives the masculine genius. This yearning for a greater, more intense flame, in many exceptional cases does not care if it is self-destructive.

And scars, skin marred with wounds past suffered,
Hypoxic from spiritual dives, water deep,
Where breath is an afterthought, long beyond reach.
The narcissistic pool from which I look into,
To revel in who I am and what I have become.
The smooth-flowing pool looks back at me.
It sees me differently, close and far.
It sees what is born from the trees and the stars.

Love, in many ways, creates a distinction between philosophy and self-help literature. The difference is significant: there is a distinction between simply improving your life and learning how to live well. Where self-help is about making your life better, and philosophy is about living well. "Better" is subjective, based on one's conditions, desires, and often the influence imposed by society. "Living well," however, is eternal. It transcends material conditions and desires. Living well is not contingent on any particular circumstance—it is a way of being, a truth that persists regardless of one's material wealth or social status. In this sense, living well is a state of mind, a profound understanding of how to engage with life meaningfully, independent of external conditions. The highest form of life is not attained through material success, but through a divine, unconditional love for life itself. The highest person is one who approaches life with unwavering love, a love that is non-negotiable and persistent in its affirmation of whatever it chooses to affirm. This person is not necessarily the most successful by conventional standards, as their actions and outcomes are not primarily related to material gain or self-preservation. Their highest form of success is found in the quality of their love and commitment to the affirmation of life.

If your goal is to achieve material success, you may need to disregard love in its purest sense. While it is certainly possible to achieve material success while maintaining love, the two must be intermeshed and used where they are components of a bigger system. Critics might argue that the billionaires of the world have achieved their success because they loved the work they did. But how do we know they truly loved it? If they had known their endeavors would yield no financial reward, would they have continued pursuing them purely out of love? Perhaps they loved the material outcomes—the wealth and success—and it was this desire for results that carried them through the inevitable ups and downs of business. Additional problems arise when connecting love with the valuations of good and bad, as a person may mistakenly tie the fluctuations in the conditions of their life to their levels of love. When experiencing a downturn in life, they might perceive a corresponding downturn in their love, leading them to feel a compulsion to escape, perhaps through substances like alcohol or even contemplating suicide. However, love itself is not bound to life's ups and downs in this way. Love is, in fact, an oppositional force to the desire for death. While drugs may serve as temporary anesthetics to mask the absence of love, love itself is not a drug. The real "drug" is anything that is not love. Love cannot be replaced or substituted by substances; they offer fleeting relief, but they do not address the deeper, more profound need for connection to life. For example, in the realm of eroticism, everything that occurs in the body in response to excitation serves the purposes of life. The excitement arises from the potential to improve life's circumstances, such as the possibility of reproduction. This is a biological mechanism deeply tied to life's continuation.

In contrast, drugs like morphine or cocaine create excitement without any external circumstance triggering it, providing a form of stimulation that bypasses life's natural challenges and rewards. This could be seen as a form of cheating life. However, avoiding the natural course of life is ultimately counterproductive. One can learn to please the giver of life or, perhaps more deeply, discover how to find life intrinsically pleasing by loving everything you continually create for yourself. The key lies not in escaping reality, but in learning to find joy and satisfaction within it, even in its imperfections.

Thoughtless,
All my poems, riddled with errors,
Without perfect rhymes, they rush in haste.
The scholars do as they do:
Overanalyze, compare meter, structure,
Calibrate rhythm. The misspellings and
Lie after lie, all the while,
There is a more concise form of expression.
shamelessly steal, slow to mature,
Slow-moving, designed for subtler eyes.
The sour flavor that hints in my water.
But my kind of work is none the worse
For any of these matters.
Not exactly bonnie, they are sae-weel strangers.
The beautiful, simple, and concise form
Is no representation of my heart.
I did not write for the sake of pushing boundaries,
Innovating, spearheading, contributing to literature.
I wrote them because I loved writing them.

MISCELLANEOUS POEMS FOUND FLOATING AT DAWN UPON THE RIVER

Beautiful, the morning pasture and its dew,
though water drops to oblivion in solitude.
From time to time, I decide
all the summer's time I could not confide.
This world is ------

You have not been given any chances?
Never been given any opportunities?
But you were selected to be alive, were you not?
Is that not already the ultimate defeat of the odds?

What an absurdity.
What an ingratitude.
Is the breath in your lungs not enough of a given chance?
Are the thoughts in your head not enough of an opportunity?

Just like heaven,
The kingdom of hell
is formed from eternal love too.

Where did she go?
I sacrificed her.
Why not take on another?
Does my solitude scare you?

Every once in a while,
A person looks at me,
See right through my body,
They see only spirit, they give a look,
as if they discovered a second moon.
those people who see spirits,
are whom I choose to surround myself with.

*I try and try again to do something productive
Show others that I am at least in first impression sane.
Every time I set up the workbench,
I get unbridled headaches and such disastrous pain,
That is until I find the right little books in which to entrench
then pound away with my silly rhymey words,
In such instance it is as if my soul is relieved from the absurd,
Like bloodied ankles unshackled from chains.*

O'ernight, discretely, under frayed shrouds,
Shadowing darkness; humid warm breezes,
Quietly whitely under the grey clouds,
The musk, it breathes, it wheezes,
The damp discomfort of the rabble,
The weird, the whole,
as droplets after long struggle,
spiritual condensate,
from vapor they turn to rain,
Should we sabor more what falls, or what remains?

Oh, but one day splitting the sky in two,
The cracking lightning bolt furiously strikes true,
In the sweetest moments, we will see every shade of blue
Oh, but one day the sky will light anew,
From the vapor they turn to rain,
And the sky will tighten his grip again.

My brother, look at the fabric,
Look at the golden cloth threaded upon our skins,
Whether impetuously or in wait,
through inheritance or seizure,
It all in the end belongs to us as kings.

Time, O Time,
Reliance upon thee;
As once stopped,
Existence ceases to be.

Every new chapter and stage,
Existence is perpetually
Thrust into the strange.
We are wholly and pitifully
Reliant upon constant, unending change.

Time, O Time,
Dependence upon thee—
Everything of great splendor
Affirms your necessity.

*In the night, it is so easy
To see the souls bustle about,
To see the glistening stars—
I could not believe
The whole time they were so bright.*

*For the night is when dim spirits kindle,
They flash sparks with liquor's spindle.
But I care not for the common stars,
I care not for the lesser souls.*

*For that, I much prefer the daylight—
It drowns them all out,
And filters what my attention deserves.*

The loud crows
    Of my fathers and mentors
    Have dimmed
The inner glow of my heart.

The solitude is everything,
    To heal the chords,
    Back to their start,
I can finally hear the keys and hammers.
    Drips of my tears,
    how they roll down,
    The soft melodic splatter drowns
    The springs and their sounds.
So I wipe them off quickly,
    Before they hit the ground.

What a profound lie life is,
Beautiful too, unique.
Drives nothing beyond it to speak,
Nothing to disprove,
For it has no underlying truth.
The lie sits around waiting
In its shoddy kissing booth.

You can only love or hate it,
Pass by or pay for your kisses.
Some do not like the price, so they end chaste.
I admit it may be an error to arrive at derision in haste.
However, there is no real correct decision to make,
Just, if you choose to leave, do it yourself.
Don't try to make me join you.

So many drowning, drowning around me.
If you so much as help one,
They will drown you too in this sea.
They splatter and splinter about,
So anxiously, so inefficiently.
And when you point to their errors,
They give you a look and ask what it matters.

Sooner or later,
Their legs give in from treading any longer.
They sink down half-heartedly,
Begging to go on just a little further.
What they beg for, I do not know.
Maybe for forgiveness of sins from some time ago?
Consequences are from errors, not from sins.
Ignorance is the true sickness that affects therein.
Burning are their legs as the oxygen subsides,
Fading from their eyes and dimming their sight.
Then they will say it was all meaningless—
Only the best dramatics to rationalize their mess.

Thank goodness for the water and the splendid sea,
It has been nothing but a rich and welcoming home to me.
Well maybe it comes second to the shaded peace under the willow or apple tree.
Either way both are truly beautiful homes indeed.

The unworthy, the superfluous,
give them everything,
they repay me half,
insidious, unscrupulous,
When the rocks on my back double,
their snickering laughs see no trouble.
They move about knowing only
the carrot and the whip,
and they shall never feel my true friendship.

I have never been one to criticize
Another's lust
It would be hypocritical first
For those that know me,
Secondly,
How is there no love in lust?
It makes no sense you see
What can the desire come from
if not love's eternal glory.

*Fighting death,
constant all throughout life.
Siguiendo luchando,
porque mi amor es fuerte.*

*You may know rivers,
but I know of famines—
From the fields of Ireland
to the dust-choked plains.*

*One Rabbit, the fertile Bay of Bengal,
pestilence cycling over the steppes,
China, Holodomor, Ethiopia, Chalisa—
echoes of hunger's hollowing tests.*

*Who thinks of when the waters stop, its effects?
Where are your rivers in the frigid cold?
The neglect. My soul has grown weary of famines—
long forgotten, yet in my body, memory holds.*

Letter To Byron's Daughter,

The One in Italy.

You will have eaten to you fill,
Sooner than I taste a floors crumb
For my love knows not equal still
Making envious eyes bare down from heaven's hill
You make the sun so naturally turn to dawn
Tore down all I knew to be birthed of passion

Oh, do I see the jealousness of divine light
Reflect upon your most passing expressions
With every ounce of all my might
With every penny that crosses my path
I will pay to keep you in my sight
And hold you dearly as if it was my last,

And your eyes so brilliant their shade of blue
Why should I live without them to look into
What am I worth; What point has time.
If you cannot feel my heart's burning hearth
And if you cannot have all that I can assign.

*Como tú, no hay ninguna.
Si no puedo decírtelo, se lo a la luna.*

Much time it took to solve,
The swollen body and chronic stress,
Time too, for my mind to find much needed rest,
Not easy to transform from knowing
Action only at another's behest,
To find mine own will,
To finally enjoying a psyche strong sturdy, and still
Tell me, how can one invent if nature herself a wheel,
There will always be danger to consider,
But danger deserves my contempt
as long as I can heal!

*What has come from rational thought
And all the straightforward logical remarks,
But the erroneous formalization
Of what we knew from the start?
The world chooses to exist from emotion,
And all that is correct comes from the heart.*

Where does the craving come from to uncover the mask, rather than make it beautiful?

Kto ma szczęście w kartach, nie ma szczęścia w miłości.

Worrying about exaltation
Is a poet's dilemma.
It is still another fixed fetter,
Another bondage
A man must surpass.

*My life is a value exchange.
Not only does life give me so much,
but I also give oh so much back.
For without me who else
would write this poetry.
NEVER forget the exchange is **equal**.*

If I am not given, then I will take.
If others do not want what I can give,
Then it will be given to the gods.

What a blessing, a good sacrifice.
When the higher receives it cares not
how it was acquired.

*I know many a maddened stare, but one special there
lies the Anti-Orpheus laughing at your despair.
Withheld from all beauty and earthly gifts,
nothing can be taken, as nothing was his.
Never knowing the underworld,
never knowing love's kiss,
never experiencing any hints of bliss.*

THE LOVIST

Investigations and Poetry on Love and Death

Evan Costa

CITATIONS

[1] Wiener, Malcolm H. "The collapse of civilizations." Belfer Center for Science and International Affairs. Harvard Kennedy School Paper (2018): 1-22.

[2] Bianchine, Peter J., and Thomas A. Russo. "The role of epidemic infectious diseases in the discovery of America." Allergy and Asthma Proceedings. Vol. 13. No. 5. OceanSide Publications, 1992.

[3] Nicolas Baumard, Elise Huillery, Alexandre Hyafil, Lou Safra. The cultural evolution of love in literary history. Nature Human Behaviour, 2022, 6 (4), pp.506-522. ff10.1038/s41562-022-01292-zff. ffhal-03860431v2f

[4] Gottschall, Jonathan, and Marcus Nordlund. "Romantic love: A literary universal?." Philosophy and Literature 30.2 (2006): 450-470.

[5] Lomas, Tim. "The flavours of love: A cross-cultural lexical analysis." *Journal for the Theory of Social Behaviour* 48.1 (2018): 134-152.

[6] Zamim, M., & Sahari, Y. (2020). A Contrastive Analysis of the Use of Love Expressions in Arabic and English. *International Journal of Science and Research (IJSR)*, 9(6), 332-336.

[7] HASSAN, WALAA. "EXPRESSING THE L WORD IN ARABIC." *LINGUISTICS AND LANGUAGE II* (2015): 76.

[8] M, R., & P, V. (2022). The elements of love in the Kurunthogai. *International Research Journal of Tamil*, 4(S-21), 639-643. https://doi.org/10.34256/irjt224s2180

[9] Morris, J. A. (1989). THE STRUCTURE OF" LOVE" IN THE LITERATURE AND THE LIFE OF JAPAN AND THE WEST: An Interdisciplinary Analysis of the Characteristics of Love in Two Cultures. 関西大学東西学術研究所紀要, 22, A27-A81

[10] Mania, Joanna, Dick Smakman, and Tessa Verhoef. "Love in Polish and Dutch: A Cultural-Linguistic Perspective."

[11] Caldwell-Harris, C., Kronrod, A., & Yang, J. (2013). Do more, say less: Saying "I love you" in Chinese and American cultures. Intercultural Pragmatics, 10(1), 41-69.

[12] Okodia Translatins (2024, February 21). 20 words in different languages which speak of love that you probably don't know: Okodia. Agencia de traducción - Empresa de traducción. https://www.okodia.co.uk/20-words-in-different-languages-

which-speak-of-love-that-you-probably-dont-know/

ABOUT THE AUTHOR

Evan Costa

I am an engineer, traveler, entrepreneur, artist, and fairly well rounded nerd. Gotham born, South Florida raised, and Midwest educated. I took up philosophy as a bucket list item, but ended finding those philosophers are the only ones with real sense about them. Philosophy has this way of freeing you, and the strongest chains always are of the mind. In between the lines of my philosophy notes I wrote poetry. Some of the poems needed explanations, and that conceived what was ultimately birthed into this book, as my hidden love child. Whether the child has turned ugly or beautiful is not my problem. That is the child's problem.

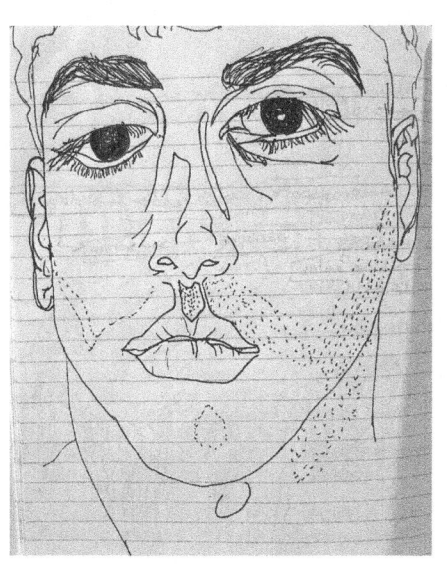

Made in the USA
Monee, IL
21 February 2025